How to Beat the I.R.S. at Its Own Game

Strategies to Avoid--and Survive--an Audit

How to Beat the I.R.S. at Its Own Game

Strategies to Avoid--and Survive--an Audit

By Amir D. Aczel, Ph.D.

Four Walls Eight Windows, New York

Published in the United States by:
Four Walls Eight Windows
39 West 14th Street, room 503
New York, N.Y., 10011

First printing November 1994.

Library of Congress Cataloging-in-Publication Data:
Aczel, Amir D.
How to beat the I.R.S. at its own game: Strategies to avoid--and survive--an audit/ by Amir D. Aczel.
p. cm.
ISBN: 1-56858-013-4 (paper)
1. Tax auditing--United States--Popular works. I. Title.
KF6314.Z9A29 1994
344.7304--dc20 94-11051
[347 3044] CIP

10 9 8 7 6 5 4 3 2 1

Printed in the United States
Text design by Kelvin Graphics U.S., Inc.

FOR MIRIAM

PREFACE

On an unusually sunny, almost warm, February afternoon in Boston in 1991, I came home early from work. I was eager to run upstairs and hug our little baby, Miriam, not yet a year old. But before doing so, I stopped for a moment to open our mailbox. And there it was—the letter from the IRS. That letter was to change my life. For the next two years, my wife Debra and I had no peace. And Miriam had to learn to walk among high piles of receipts and forms strewn all over our apartment floor, her parents spending hours sifting through the piles for a receipt or document the insatiable auditor decided he wanted to see that particular week of the many weeks of the audit. Agent L.G. did not believe in courtesy or patience or human decency. He routinely demanded that we report at his office at 8 AM, knowing full well that our baby sitter only came at 9. He would repeatedly call us at home, waking us up at 5 AM on the day of our appointment to tell us that he was ill, and demand to reschedule. I now know that many of his practices were even against the IRS' own regulations for its auditors. For the longest time, we had no idea why we were chosen for the audit. "Why us?" was a question we asked ourselves almost every day.

Trying to answer this question was what finally helped bring about the end of our audit, and—more importantly— led to the research that produced this book. The audit was getting worse, and L.G. was demanding more and more information, more canceled checks, receipts, letters from employers, documents, more time.... In trying desperately to understand exactly what it was the IRS was after in an audit, I turned to the one thing I know best: statistics. Thinking about this problem in an objective and non-personal way, I began to realize that the reason for almost every audit by the IRS had to be statistics. Since this was *my* area, and since I believed that I was better at it than the many statisticians employed by the IRS, I knew that I could beat them. My ensuing research on the IRS confirmed that I was right, and that I have even identified correctly the exact method used by the agency in determining who should be audited: discriminant analysis. The statistics textbook I had written a few years earlier included almost an entire chapter on this important technique. Soon it further occurred to me that I could actually use the IRS' own technique of discriminant analysis to defeat its use by IRS employees. The scheme was easy; all I needed now was a few hundred tax returns.

I began to ask around. I found out that I was not alone, and that many in my category—professionals, independent contractors, small business owners, anyone who does not file the simplest tax form—get audited. And I discovered that audit victims (as well as other taxpayers) will sometimes agree to share their information with you if you can offer them a scientific way to avoid the torment in the future. Within a few months, I had a small data set of 32 individual tax returns, eighteen of which had been audited. I learned a lot from this initial group of returns, since in analyzing them I was using the same technique used by the perpetrators of the audits.

As my queries expanded, I made contact with a considerable number of tax professionals nationwide. I used mailing lists of professional accounting organizations, friends' recommendations, and the Yellow Pages in locating a representative sample of CPAs and Enrolled Agents from every state. I spent hours phoning, faxing, and writing these professionals. They provided me with a wealth of information on tax preparation and audits, and I am indebted to these people for sharing their time and experience with me. Twenty-eight of these tax professionals volunteered to send me copies of tax returns of audited and unaudited clients (about half from each group) on the condition that these be confidential— with no names, social security numbers, or any other identifying information. Within eighteen months of starting this research project, I had amassed an impressive sample of 1,289 tax returns: 631 of which had been audited and the rest (the control group) not. Now I was finally on my way. After using my own discriminant analysis to separate the audits from the non-audits in my sample, I went on to devise a more powerful methodology. I needed to estimate with great accuracy exactly what it was that caused a tax return to be audited. Eventually, an artificial-intelligence algorithm which I programmed on a Cray-2 supercomputer gave me the perfect results I needed.

As I learned more, I became smarter about our own continuing audit. Our taxes are complicated. Since I am both a professor and an author, and since my wife also works, our tax return includes both a Schedule A and a Schedule

C. From my exciting research findings, I was able to pinpoint exactly what it was that our auditor was after. Armed with this knowledge—and the sophistication gained from having looked at so many audits and talked with so many tax professionals—my wife and I were able to take control of our case. As a final result, the IRS determined that *they* owed us money!

Hearing the story of my audit and the unusual research I conducted, the co-publishers of Four Walls Eight Windows, John Oakes and Dan Simon, were quick to understand the importance of my conclusions for virtually all taxpayers. They provided me with constant encouragement throughout the project of writing this book. The results of my exhaustive study of exactly what it is that causes a taxpayer's audit is the subject of *How to Beat the I.R.S. at Its Own Game*. Read it, it will save you from the ordeal.

CHAPTER 1

WHY YOU NEED THIS BOOK

O ver a million people are audited by the IRS each year. While this number represents only about one percent of all individual taxpayers, certain groups—professionals with business and other expenses, the self employed, and others— have a disproportionately high rate of selection for an audit.

The IRS selects you for an audit based purely on *statistical* considerations, and not because it knows that you did something "wrong." If the IRS computer determines that you look—statistically—like the type of person who, in the past, has tended to yield more money for the government as a result of an audit, then you will be audited!

An IRS audit is one of the most unpleasant experiences imaginable, and you will want to avoid it if at all possible. I know. I experienced one. Even if you were extremely careful in preparing your return, chances are you will have to pay additional tax following an audit. And with these added taxes come penalties, and interest at a rate that if charged by someone else would be considered usurious. To add to your pain, the IRS keeps your interest clock ticking even while your case remains open due to *their* bureaucracy and no fault of your own.

The fact is that less than fifteen percent of all audits by the IRS result in a draw or in a refund to you. The rest—over 85%—

result in additional tax assessments. And the average amount of additional tax assessed is much larger than the average refund. The total amount of money the government gains from IRS audits each year is in the *billions* while the total amount refunded due to audits is only in the millions. Even if you end up among the lucky few who do get a refund, the amount will not begin to compensate you for the aggravation of having had an IRS agent intimidate you, scrutinize every detail of your financial life, and invade your privacy.

Surprisingly, very little has been written on how to avoid an IRS audit. The main reason for this is that the government guards the secret statistical formula—the equation the computer uses in determining whom to select for an audit—more closely than it guards military secrets. It is believed that only a handful of people within the giant IRS bureaucracy know the actual formula that determines audits.

The IRS gains tremendously from distrusting you and conducting these audits. Almost every year, the IRS Commissioner goes to Congress to ask for additional millions of dollars to pay for increased audits, promising in return billions in additional tax collection. Where does the money come from? The IRS tells us that only five percent of taxpayers cheat on their returns. And yet the majority of audits produce extra tax revenues! Much of the money is obtained from you *not* because you cheated on your taxes and were caught, but rather because the burden of proof for every single item on your tax return lies squarely on you.

In the audit, IRS agents aggressively try to disallow whatever they can, so that anything you cannot prove to *their* absolute satisfaction is held against you. In the eyes of your IRS case officer, you are guilty even before the audit begins. Almost all audits end with at least some disallowance of your claims. Afterwards, the IRS determines the adjustments needed in your tax bill based on the disallowances, and you pay. You will likely have to pay added tax and interest even if you appeal or go to court, and the amounts are not small. A 1988 study by the GAO (the government's General Accounting Office) has found that in over half the cases, IRS agents incorrectly assessed higher taxes in their audits (see Schnepper, 1994, in the Bibliography). Table 1 below shows average additional tax payments resulting from I.R.S. audits, for all states, in decreasing order.

Table 1
Average Audit-Resulting Payments

Colorado	$17,802	Hawaii	$3,892
Texas	$9,790	Delaware	$3,756
Alaska	$8,985	Georgia	$3,787
Maryland(&DC)	$7,532	Kentucky	$3,713
Oklahoma	$7,382	Virginia	$3,660
Arkansas	$7,318	New Mexico	$3,590
Florida	$7,289	Ohio	$3,584
Nevada	$6,570	Wisconsin	$3,382
New Jersey	$6,390	N. Carolina	$3,286
Idaho	$6,295	S. Carolina	$3,209
New York	$6,290	Washington	$3,188
Massachusetts	$5,798	Indiana	$3,180
California	$5,608	Maine	$3,069
Oregon	$5,561	Iowa	$3,049
Illinois	$5,188	Rhode Island	$2,965
Kansas	$4,901	Minnesota	$2,949
Pennsylvania	$4,670	Missouri	$2,922
Utah	$4,372	Nebraska	$2,728
Michigan	$4,315	S. Dakota	$2,629
Arizona	$4,296	Mississippi	$2,529
Tennessee	$4,199	Alabama	$2,513
Wyoming	$4,154	W. Virginia	$2,375
Louisiana	$4,140	Montana	$2,181
New Hampshire	$3,983	Vermont	$2,095
Connecticut	$3,889	N. Dakota	$1,825

(Source: Internal Revenue Service)

3

The fact that the IRS uses a secret formula makes us all victims of statistics. The secrecy of the formula used to determine who is audited assures the IRS that one of two things will happen. Either, for fear of an audit, you will claim on your return less than the amount to which you are entitled—thus paying more tax than necessary right when you file—or, you may exceed the invisible line in the secret formula and have to pay more tax after they audit you. Either way, you lose. This is the "Catch 22" that works so well for the IRS in their game against you, the taxpayer. Is there anything you can do?

Luckily, you have me! Tax problems have been looked at by accountants and tax lawyers and they are the ones who give advice and write books on how to prepare your taxes. As you see, however, the problem of avoiding an audit is a *statistical* one. As a statistician and the author of a number of books and research articles on statistics, I decided to take on the IRS and to beat them at their own nasty, unfair game of statistics. The Internal Revenue Service employs scores of its own statisticians, working hard on their side to devise new ways to increase audit revenues. I wanted to find a way to help you keep those hard-earned dollars so that you will never again have to pay more taxes than you actually owe.

I conducted a careful analysis of thousands of bits of information derived from a large random sample of actual returns of people who were audited and people who were not audited. As a research statistician working on the leading edge of this science, I have continuous access to methodologies and powerful supercomputers. My statistical methods (which are about 15 years ahead of those currently in use by the IRS) easily cracked the secret IRS audit formula.

I was able to piece together a close picture of the actual secret code, a *rule* that statistically separated the returns in my sample known to have been audited by the IRS from those returns known not to have been audited. Then I tested the formula against other actual returns and was able to predict with great accuracy (over 90%) whether or not a return was audited.

This confirmed that I have estimated the correct formula.

In the first few chapters of the book, I describe how the IRS operates. I then describe the audit process and give you some advice on what to do—and, often more important—what *not* to do in case you are audited. I discuss the secret formula and how the IRS uses it against you, and explain its reconstruction later in the book. The remaining chapters explain in simple terms how you can benefit from my estimated formula by using simple rules to test whether your return is likely to be audited. I show you how to prepare and file your return in a way that will maximize the amount of money to which you are entitled while minimizing the chances of an IRS audit. No one else can give you such advice. After reading this book you will never again throw away money that is rightfully yours just because you are afraid of being audited. And on the other hand, you will not file a return that instantly begs the IRS computer to pick you for an audit. Of course I need to caution you that *statistics* is the name of the game. So if you follow my advice you will minimize the *chance* of an audit. I cannot give you a guarantee that you will not be audited. Returns are audited for a variety of reasons—some of which are totally out of your control or mine. But if you follow my advice, the chances of an audit will be much reduced and you will be much farther ahead in this game. Let's even the playing field!

CHAPTER 2

A GOLIATH NAMED I.R.S.

Y ou've been sitting in the stuffy, windowless room on the 13th floor of the Federal Building for three hours now, and the end is nowhere in sight. The gruff, middle-aged IRS agent sitting across the table has been endlessly writing things down on a yellow legal pad while referring again and again to copies of the bank statements you had to ask your bank to provide you for the audit (at a cost of $144.00!—you didn't know you had to keep the original statements they send you...). Every once in a while, the agent breaks his pencil (he must be really out to get you), stands up and deliberately walks over to the rusty pencil sharpener on the wall, the sound of which is beginning to give you the worst headache of your life. Eventually— weeks, perhaps months later—you end up paying lots of money as well. The agent could not balance your check-book to his satisfaction. You had made deposits of amounts in cash, mostly reimbursed job-related expenses, but the agent doesn't take your word for it. He claims all the deposits were unreported "income." Income from *what*? You work for a salary. But it's your word against his, and there is no "innocent until proven guilty" assumption in the audit process. You appeal and lose, and you worry that a tax court may not rule in your favor. You settle and pay tax you don't owe on income you never had and pray to have this nightmare end. Then the IRS tells you they want to look at other tax years you filed.... You have become a victim of a vicious audit. Your crime was carelessness. Did all this have to happen? I imagine that psychiatrists who treat patients for post-audit trauma report the first question asked by the victims is: "Why me?"

With close to 120,000 employees, the Internal Revenue Service is the largest agency of the U.S. Government. This should come as no surprise, considering that the IRS brings in yearly revenues of about a trillion dollars.

The Service is headquartered in Washington and is headed by a Commissioner who is appointed by the President. The country is divided into seven regions, each headed by an IRS Regional Commissioner, who is also a political appointee. There is a further division into 63 Districts, each headed by a Director. Then there are ten Service Centers (Fresno, Ogden, Austin, Philadelphia, Atlanta, Hotsville, Andover, Cincinnati, Memphis), where you send your tax return each year. It is at one of these Service Centers that the processing of your tax return—and potential trouble—begins.

The information in your return is keypunched for entry into the big IRS computer located in West Virginia. Because of the large total number of returns filed each year (about 200,000,000—including individual, corporate, and other returns), the IRS has to hire many temporary workers as keypunch operators during the busiest time, from January through April. These operators are poorly trained, overworked, and paid minimum wage. Since they are tired

THE IRS IS THIS COUNTRY'S LARGEST BUREAUCRACY A GIANT WHOSE SOLE PURPOSE IS TO COLLECT MONEY

7

TEN PERCENT OF
ALL RETURNS
ARE ENTERED
INCORRECTLY
INTO THE IRS
COMPUTER

and careless and have to process such a huge number of returns in limited time, many errors occur. As many as ten percent of all returns they enter are in error because of the carelessness of the keypunch operators—and these errors by IRS employees could result in your being audited.

Your return, possibly already in error, now goes into the central IRS computer in West Virginia. The computer is central to all IRS activity. This fact cannot be overstated in trying to understand the mentality of the organization.

Virtually everyone at the IRS, from the Commissioner down, worships The Computer—sometimes forgetting that *people* program the computer as well as enter data into it. The computer crashed in 1985, and by the IRS's own admission, many millions in tax revenue were lost forever.

The digital villain now starts to work on your return. The first thing the computer does is to check your Social Security number (SSN). The IRS identifies you, not by name or any other means, but by your SSN. If you (or the Service Center keypunchers) entered the wrong SSN for you, your joint filer, or a dependent, the machine will catch the error and spew out your return for examination (this does not mean an audit—not yet, at least). Next, the computer looks for obvious things that computing machines were designed for—arithmetic errors.

An arithmetic error will also cause your return to be tagged for examination by an IRS employee, and usually you will then be contacted by mail to resolve the problem. An audit by mail is—usually—not a big deal, as you can resolve the mathematical error with the IRS quickly and without adversity. Some even say that an arithmetic error reduces your chance for a "real" audit as it tags your return and kicks it out of the system for some time, but there is no actual proof of this theory.

A related issue is the "nice-numbers trap." If the IRS employee who looks at your return once it has been identified by the computer sees expenses or other numbers that look "too nice to be real": $15,000, or $29,000 (rather than: $14,987.56, or $28,759.12, for example), then this suspicion may result in an audit. It should be noted that while most audits are indeed triggered by the computer, a small percentage of all audits (about five percent) are caused by other factors. One of these factors is information provided to the IRS by people who claim to have knowledge about your financial life.

The next step in the computer check is a matching program. Here all the financial information that is reported about you from institutions and employers on forms 1099 and W-2 is matched against what you have reported yourself on the return. Any mismatched information will cause your return to be pulled out by the computer for an audit, at least by mail.

Assuming you have passed all these tests by the computer, your return now faces the big IRS acid test: the Discriminant Function (which the IRS abbreviates as "DIF"). Here the computer constructs your *statistical profile*. What is this statistical profile, and why is it needed? In theory, the principle is as follows. The IRS does not know whether or not you paid your taxes to the full extent of the law, or whether you cheated. So it wants to *compare* you, statistically, with the group of people that it

9

believes cheat on their taxes. If you look, statistically, like the people in that group (that is, you have an income level similar to theirs, and you have deductions in the same categories and in similar proportions to the "bad guys," and you have other characteristics in common with them, such as your profession)—then, chances are, you cheat as well. Therefore, goes the IRS logic, you too should be audited. This is the IRS reasoning that underlies the entire process and presumes your guilt even before an actual examination begins!

In reality, this is of course quite possibly not the case. The reason is very simple. In many cases, *nobody* knows for sure whether a person cheated on his or her taxes. Why? The following fact should be quite convincing. Every year, *Money* magazine asks a group of 50 top national tax experts to prepare the return of a hypothetical individual, and then they publish the comparison of the experts' results. In all the years this has been done, not a single time have even two of the experts agreed on the exact amount of tax due! This example, as well as inherent vagueness in the thousands of pages of tax law, court rulings and precedents, shows that it is virtually impossible to say whether or not an actual individual pays the full amount of tax due. (Note that here we are not talking about criminal cases, tax evasion and fraud.)

What is the *reality* then? In reality, the IRS doesn't know (or even care) whether or not you cheated—they are simply concerned with the issue: can we get more money from this individual? And this is the key to the Secret Formula, the DIF. The IRS has *past records* of people whose audits resulted in additional tax due (actually the information is based on relatively small samples of people selected purely at random every three years and investigated thoroughly). The DIF, then, is a rule that *discriminates* between those people from whom the IRS was able in the past to squeeze more money in audits, and those from whom the IRS could not get more money. The DIF contains variables that are based on your income, your expenses, your deductions. If the combination of factors in the formula makes you look like a potential milk cow for more tax dollars, the IRS will audit you.

THE DIF IS THE COMPUTER FORMULA THAT LOOKS FOR RETURNS OF TAXPAYERS WHO STATISTICALLY YIELD MORE MONEY WHEN AUDITED

About *ten percent* of all individual returns are selected for audit by the DIF. Once this happens, IRS employees (Classifiers/Screeners) manually scan these returns tagged by the computer, and audits actually occur for about ten percent of the returns selected by the machine. This fact—that only ten percent of the DIF-selected returns are actually audited—will be quite useful for us later in constructing audit-proofing strategies.

Let's return to the IRS system. If you were not selected for an audit, the IRS continues processing your return. If you owe taxes your check will be cashed rather quickly, and if you are due a refund, one will be sent to you. If you are selected for an audit, your file is sent to your local District Office. The Examination Division in the District Office will then contact you, usually by letter, for an Office Audit. Or a Field Audit may be conducted—at your place of business or residence. The District Office also has a Collection Division, responsible for getting the money from you following an audit, a Criminal Investigation Division, and a Problem Resolution Office. In the next chapter we discuss how the people of the IRS view you, the taxpayer.

CHAPTER 3

HOW THE IRS VIEWS YOU, THE TAXPAYER

There is an old Yiddish joke about the guy who comes home and cheerfully tells his wife: "Honey, the doctor examined me thoroughly and found nothing wrong! I'm as healthy as can be." "What?" says his wife, "Surely he didn't examine you well enough, or else he would have found *something* wrong with you!"

In the eyes of the IRS, there is something wrong with each and every one of us taxpayers. The mission of the IRS is to find out just what it is. This notion is clearly implied in Section 4325 of the official *Internal Revenue Manual*, 132-1 (4-11-80):

> It has been indicated that, where a regular or normal tax examination ends, an in-depth examination should begin.

This means: believe no one! Search hard enough and you will find something. Other official IRS guidelines to its agents describe methods of putting the audited individual on the defensive, using intimidation and psychological pressure, and pursuing the case until weaknesses eventually appear, which can then be exploited for more money. The IRS is able to assume you are guilty because you are not (at least not yet) accused in court of having committed a crime and thus would enjoy the assumption of innocence.

THE IRS VIEWS EVERY SINGLE TAXPAYER AS A POTENTIAL TAX CHEATER

This is a very tricky point. The IRS always assumes that you are guilty of something, and the auditor tries to find that "something." In fact, the actual reason for the computer's having chosen you for an audit based on the secret formula is not known to the auditor! The whole process is a Kafkaesque nightmare. You stand accused of something unknown to you—even unknown to your tormentors! The idea that you are innocent until proven guilty and that your guilt must be demonstrated beyond a reasonable doubt—the judicial concept that lies at the heart of the American way of life—does not apply here. Only if you are accused of a crime in a court of law will you get this basic protection, and the IRS is above the law. Even if the IRS suspects you of a crime, it will try to take away your assumption of innocence beforehand, in the audit process. Agents are trained in entrapping suspected taxpayers into an admission of guilt (thus depriving them of the *Miranda* protection). This is why it is so important to keep your cool and stay in control.

Usually, however, the audit process does not lead to criminal charges. Understand that the IRS is generally interested in one thing: more dollars. They will try to get these dollars from you by depriving you of any tax deduction they can on your return. In some cases, they will even use the implied or actual threat of criminal charges to get you to admit to owing more money. Few audits result in criminal charges of tax evasion and fewer result in prison sentences. But the threat is definitely there.

The IRS has been cultivating this atmosphere of fear for many decades. Ironically, much of the success of the IRS in spreading fear among us taxpayers is due to one individual, who was not even employed by the IRS: the gangster Al Capone. Since the successful conviction of the elusive Al Capone for tax evasion 50 years ago, the IRS has enjoyed an almost legendary aura. However innocent we may be, we have all been living with fear somewhere in the backs of our minds (rational or otherwise) of being caught in the clutches of the IRS and ending up in jail....

Since the social upheavals of the 1960s, however, this instinctive, implanted fear of the great Goliath has been on the decline. The IRS has noticed an increasing boldness on the part of the taxpayer and realized the need for new "examples." It began an active search for scapegoats. It wanted someone who was well-known, generally disliked by the public, and who would be convicted of tax evasion in a court of law and given a stiff sentence that would then serve to instill new fears in the public. After a concentrated research effort, the IRS found exactly what they were looking for in the person of Leona Helmsley. The immensely wealthy, arrogant, and oft-despised Queen of Mean, as she has been called, fit the bill very well. The government was able to prove that Helmsley was guilty of tax evasion by fraudulently deducting over a million dollars in renovation expenses for her home rather than for her hotels, as she had claimed on her tax return. She was sentenced to jail in a much-publicized trial. As if to make sure that we all paid attention, in the following years since the Helmsley trial several other wealthy, although less-known, people were sentenced to jail for tax evasion in trials that were extensively covered by the media. The doctrine of fear was on its way back. Even the President is not safe from the long arm of the IRS, as we know from news reports about Mr. Clinton's alleged underpayment of taxes many years ago.

In the eyes of the IRS we are all guilty of something. Depending on what it is that the IRS thinks we do to avoid paying the government its due, it classifies us taxpayers into three main categories: nonfiler, underreporter, overdeductor.

NONFILER

A "nonfiler" as the IRS refers to him or her, is a person who has not filed a tax return for at least one tax year. Not filing a tax return when tax is due is a crime and can lead to felony charges and jail sentences. The IRS uses computer matching techniques to catch nonfilers. If you earn wages or work as an independent contractor, documents filed with the IRS (form 1099, W-2) will be matched against your social security number and you will be caught. Only rare individuals, for example an undocumented illegal alien who earns a living in cash, can escape detection for a while. Even such a person will eventually be caught by other means. The IRS estimates that about three percent of the population are nonfilers; others believe the figure is somewhat higher.

UNDERREPORTER

"Underreporter" is how the IRS refers to a person who reports on his or her return an income that is smaller than the actual one. The underreporter is, by far, the greatest obsession of the IRS. A nonfiler is someone who doesn't report at all and can eventually be caught and made to pay up. However, those of us who do report an income to the IRS are *all* underreporters in the eyes of the Service. The greatest percentage of IRS effort concentrating on people who do file is aimed at proving underreported income.

The underreporter is the government's worst taxpaying enemy. The IRS knows that in many situations it is easy to conceal income, and this leads to the IRS' belief that all of us do it. If they shake you hard enough, you will reveal to them the source of your hidden income.

The ideal underreporter could be someone who lives in a small community that practices a barter economy. A fisherman living in Alaska gives a local artist some fish, and she, in turn, gives him a painting. No cash was transferred, no transactions recorded, and (unless someone reports them to the IRS) no one will be the wiser and this trade and its implicit incomes will forever remain untaxed.

Close to this kind of underreporter is the person who deals solely (or almost solely) in cash. Cash transactions, like barters, are almost impossible to detect. Large transactions ($10,000 or more) must be documented under government requirements, but smaller ones are not reported. Ironically, your friendly neighborhood bank is your worst enemy. Banks report interest income to the IRS. Also, as our introductory story shows, banks can be made to reveal all of your transactions. If you made money in cash but put it in your bank account, the IRS can trace the deposit. So even if your deposit was not income but of any of a million other kinds, the insatiable Goliath will claim it was income if it traces your deposit ("everyone hides income"), and charge you additional tax, interest, and penalty.

Our economy is based on bank transactions, checks, electronic transfers, credit cards, and it is moving ever faster in this direction toward a perfect recording of all your financial transactions. The information superhighway, now widely discussed in the media, will spell heaven for the IRS. In fact, the government is already pushing for the implementation of electronic devices (Clipper Chips) that will automatically decode and enable reporting of all electronic information traffic on computer networks to government agencies: the FBI, the CIA, and, yes, the IRS. Ostensibly, this cause is championed to help the government fight crime, especially drug deals, by making large cash transactions visible. In reality, the IRS will benefit most from this electronic spying.

While making our economy more efficient, electronic filing systems, banks, credit card companies, and ATMs all help the IRS because they can be easily scrutinized. In many countries in the world the economy is based much more on cash than is our own economy. It is common in such countries to see people leaving a bank with huge wads of money in their hands. Lower crime rates make this possible, and—in fact—in many of these countries as much as

60% of the economy is unreported to the government. Many people in Greece, Italy, Turkey, and other countries are extensive underreporters or nonfilers. Our modern, technologically-advanced economy makes it difficult to underreport and at the same time puts honest people under suspicion of having unreported income by tracing transactions that may not necessarily be income.

The IRS is so concerned with its hunt for hidden income that its agents will sometimes even overlook tax deductions (our next topic) that look inflated, because they are really looking for the mythical treasures of hidden income.

OVERDEDUCTOR

The overdeductor is someone who deducts against income more expenses, losses, charitable contributions, or other deductions than he or she is entitled to. High deductions figure prominently in the Secret Formula and trigger many audits. The agent conducting the audit will try to challenge the legitimacy of deductions and credits against income and will force you to give evidence to support every item. This evidence is usually in the form of receipts and other substantiation. Once you are being audited, however, more effort will still be spent on looking for that invisible unreported income.

Finally, a few words are in order about what may very well be the ugliest practice of the IRS. Like the Spanish Inquisition of the Middle Ages, the IRS encourages and actively seeks denunciations. Incredible as it may seem, the IRS will take an estranged wife's word against her husband, a husband's against his wife, a child's against his or her parents, as well as snitching by disgruntled employees or acquaintances.

There is a special telephone number for conveying the information to the IRS, and *rewards* are offered to anyone who will provide information leading to the collection of additional tax, in the form of a percentage of the amount collected. This practice opens the door to abuse and revenge by anyone who may hold a grudge against you. This is one reason why you should never discuss your taxes in casual conversation. You never know how others may view what you are saying, and what their own motives and agendas may be. The IRS policy encouraging informers brings our society closer to totalitarian regimes, where a citizen can trust no one and must watch his or her every step. Hidden enemies bent on harming you lurk everywhere. In encouraging members of the same family to inform on each other, the abhorrent IRS practice contributes directly to the breakdown of our society and its values.

THE IRS WILL REWARD ANYONE WHO WILL BETRAY YOU TO THEM

CHAPTER 4

THE DAGGER: FORMULA AND COMPUTER

I n the fall of 1943, the Germans moved into the Tuscan hill town of Santa Vittoria. The area had been controlled by the Nazis for some time, but except for stationing a few military liaison personnel in town, the occupiers let the inhabitants go about their daily lives. New information from a secret source in town, however, indicated that the villagers were hiding from their German occupiers over a million bottles of the valuable local vermouth at an undisclosed location. The military vehicles carrying several hundred soldiers into town that morning were part of an operation aimed at finding this treasure.

After the usual gentle persuasion methods failed, the Germans decided on a more extreme measure. They would randomly select a few townsfolk for a thorough investigation. These people would be tortured until they revealed the location of the town's hidden bottles—the community's only wealth. On the appointed day, Nazi soldiers patrolled the near-empty streets and found what they thought was a random sample of three people. These were carried off to a nearby cave and never heard from again. The treasure, however, was never discovered. What the

Germans did not know was that the three people they captured were not random samples. They were fascists who had been kept under house arrest by the townspeople since before the bottles were hidden; thus they did not know the hiding place. On the day the Nazi selection was made, these three were let loose by the people while everyone else stayed at home. Santa Vittoria kept its treasure.

The IRS in modern-day America has a similar treasure-hunting scheme. It is called the Taxpayer Compliance Measurement Program (TCMP). Every three years, the IRS selects a *purely random* sample of 50,000 individual taxpayers. These poor souls are treated to what accountants refer to informally as "the audit from hell."

With more than 100 million individual taxpayers nationwide, your probability of being selected—in your entire lifetime—to be among the unfortunate 50,000 chosen every three years is very small. But if you are among these people, selected for no reason but the bad luck of the draw, God help you. The IRS will not leave you alone. Auditors will want to see *everything*. This is the modern-day-American equivalent of being randomly chosen on the street for an endless session of torture when you have done absolutely nothing wrong. And your tormentors know that!

The TCMP audit will scrutinize your birth certificate, those of your family members, death certificates, marriage or divorce certificates, every bank book you ever kept, every check you have ever written, records of every bill you ever

THE TCMP IS A
POLICY OF
TORTURING THE
INNOCENT
TO GAIN
INFORMATION

21

paid, slips for every credit-card charge you ever made, the list is endless. And what you will not find in your records you will be forced to obtain from institutions, at *your* expense and your loss of valuable time. No excuse will be accepted by the IRS, and nothing will ever get you out of this terrible ordeal until the Service decides that they are finished with you. This is one case where, while you have done absolutely nothing wrong, our modern, enlightened, human-rights-conscious system will offer you no protection whatsoever.

NOTHING IS SACRED IN A TCMP AUDIT

The TCMP is a government program of relentless pressure mounted against an innocent individual for the purpose of extracting *statistical* information about an entire society. What is truly amazing about this despicable misuse of statistics is that it is perfectly legal for our government do it. The IRS tries to use the information it obtains from the TCMP sample to uncover our collective treasure—more money in the form of additional tax to be reaped from future audits that will be based on the information extracted from the TCMP. Let us see how this is done.

The principle of statistical inference is a simple one. You can gain information about a very large population (even an "infinite" population, as statisticians refer to it) by selecting a *random sample* from the population and measuring some characteristic of interest. Election-year polls, as well as the many other polls reported in the media almost daily, demonstrate this principle. Polling organizations such as Gallup will often select a random sample of 1,000 people and find out how many people in the sample have a certain characteristic, say, an intention to vote for a particular candidate. The result of the survey of only 1,000 people or so can then be extended to the entire population using statistical inference. The polling organization will state that in the entire voting population, a given percentage will vote for the candidate, plus or minus some margin of error that will typically be 2 or 3 percent. Amazingly, even a relatively small sample of 1,000 people can reveal much information, and have a small margin of error when applied to the entire population. This is a remarkable fact and demonstrates the power of statistics and how it can be used effectively to gain information.

Exactly the same principle works in the TCMP. The IRS wants to learn about the population of taxpayers. Since not every taxpayer can be examined (this would take forever), a random sample is selected. In statistical terms, a sample of 50,000 taxpayers is huge. It is definitely much larger than would be required by modern statistical theory, and it demonstrates the excesses of government and the very low value it places on our right not to be harassed.

The auditors who carry out the TCMP examinations are concerned with an important *classification* problem: they are attempting to break down the population of taxpayers into two groups—the group that can yield more money following an audit and the group that cannot. The statistical procedure that does the trick is called *discriminant analysis*. The principle of statistical inference then assures the auditors that whatever they find in the random sample can be inferred to apply very closely to the entire population—consisting of over 115 million individual taxpayers.

DISCRIMINANT
ANALYSIS IS
SUPPOSED TO
SEGMENT THE
POPULATION
INTO TWO
GROUPS: ONE
BELIEVED TO BE
HONEST, THE
OTHER
TAX-EVADING

The breakdown of the random sample into two groups is achieved by a *discriminant function.* The very thorough audit of the sample of 50,000 reveals the information on income, deductions, expenses, losses, contributions that the IRS believes will discriminate between the honest, fully-tax-paying people and the people who hide their income and overstate their deductions. Each piece of information is coded as a variable in the discriminant function, and the computer then searches for the combination of variables that will achieve the best possible discrimination between the two groups. The IRS makes no secret of its use of a "secret formula" to determine audits. Publicizing this very fact is yet another tool to intimidate us taxpayers. Here is Big Brother, spying on us with his secret formula that will tell him right away who's been naughty and who's been good. The IRS even implies that the secret formula, the DIF, is a very "complicated" equation that contains all kinds of information about us and can reveal what we do very accurately. My results of the analysis of a large sample of audited and unaudited returns paints a different picture. The number of significant variables in the IRS's DIF is probably relatively small. My study revealed that a handful of variables, all of them ratios, account for 90% of all the audits.

Once the IRS completes the TCMP analysis, the rule it extracts from the discriminant analysis becomes, by the principles of statistical inference, the actual Secret Formula of the IRS, the DIF used in determining all future audits. Long before the IRS actually sees your return, they have already made up their minds—based solely on the characteristics of *other* people—whether they will let your claims stand as they are, or doom you to an audit. They've got your number!

Chapter 4

24

CHAPTER 5

BATTLE OF THE STATISTICIANS

F rom a statistical point of view, the DIF is not the most sophisticated program available today and it makes big errors for a variety of technical reasons. Discriminant analysis was developed in 1936 by the great British statistician Sir Ronald A. Fisher (1890-1962), as a statistical classification method. The technique requires particular assumptions, such as a *normal* distribution. In the case of the IRS, many of the underlying assumptions are severely violated. For one thing, none of the variables the IRS uses are normally distributed. For another, over the years the IRS has completely distorted the discriminant procedure in its pursuit to adapt it specifically to tax audits.

The pure statistical method, derived from theory, requires the discriminant score to be a number between -1 and 1, negative numbers implying membership in one group ("audit"), and positive ones in the other ("no audit"). In their frenzy to computerize and to capitalize on as many pieces of information as possible, IRS statisticians have changed the discriminant procedure so much that now it doesn't even resemble the original, correct method. It is now a *quantitative* classification rather than a qualitative one (audit-no audit). What they do is to use (*misuse*) the DIF so it will give every taxpayer an actual *score*. This score is then used similarly to the old draft lottery. All taxpayers are rank-ordered by their DIF-scores from largest to smallest and the allotted number of audits for the year is obtained by counting down from the top—the highest DIF-score to the lowest. The statistical underpinnings for this procedure are dubious at best.

From a *moral* point of view, however, the procedure is an utter disgrace. You have done nothing wrong, but you happen to be a physician. Or a waiter/waitress, or a building contractor, or a professor. This alone will give you a high DIF score. Add the usual expenses and other characteristics that go with your profession, and chances are you will be audited. And you'll have to pay.

YOU MAY BE AUDITED AGAIN AND AGAIN JUST BECAUSE THE COMPUTER THINKS YOU LOOK LIKE SOMEONE WHO MIGHT UNDERPAY INCOME TAX

The system discriminates against certain types of professions and other taxpayer characteristics. It tries to find soft areas where added tax revenues may be extracted, with no direct concern for whether or not the tax is actually owed. If your statistical profile is similar to people who yield more tax on examination, you are a good target for an audit. Incidentally, discriminant analysis (in its original, undistorted form) is also used by banks to determine whether you are to be classified as a "good" or a "bad" credit risk. If you are classified as bad, you will be denied a loan. Recent litigation has challenged banks' use of this analysis as unfair, but don't try to complain to the IRS about using their beloved and greatly altered DIF.

The DIF is the result of a constant search by the IRS statisticians over decades. This search lacks theory because of the alterations the IRS has made in accepted statistical methods in their quest to adapt the discriminant analysis to their particular use. For this crucial drive to extract billions in extra revenues, the IRS has a very large division of statisticians to do battle with us all. The division is called Statistics of Income (SOI). The SOI employs people whose sole purpose, day after day, is to find ways of identifying those of us who can be squeezed for more dollars once our returns are examined.

The theory behind all this madness is a cynical one. Remember that by far the greatest obsession of the IRS is hidden income. Truly hidden income is impossible to find. There is absolutely nothing on a taxpayer's return that would indicate *directly* the existence of hidden income. Hence the absurdity of the SOI operation. The division is on a constant statistical search for the perfect profile of the person who hides income. The main assumption is the following: Bad people hide income. Bad people are also greedy. Therefore, these people will not only hide their income, but they will also do other things—things that will be obvious to us from their tax returns. In addition to hiding their income, these people will also exaggerate their deductions, credits, and other characteristics that will make them easy to catch. Thus, the SOI statisticians are on a constant lookout for methods of finding these telltale signs on returns. The DIF is just the mechanism for searching for the signs.

THE MAIN PURPOSE OF THE DIF IS TO MYSTERIOUSLY LEAD THE IRS TO THE TREASURES OF HIDDEN INCOME

Every year, the American Statistical Association holds its national meeting at a different location. These meetings are attended by many in the profession—mostly academics and statistical practitioners in business and industry. The national meetings act as clearing houses in the market place of ideas. Here the state of the art is explored; new methods are presented and explained; and ideas are exchanged.

Every year, the SOI division of the IRS sends a disproportionately high number of its staff to flood these meetings. While academics and statisticians in industry present new papers with important results that expand the profession, the SOI people do not. They make minimal contributions to the meetings in the form of elementary presentations of obvious (and often incorrect) statistical uses. Their sole purpose in attending these meetings is to spy! These IRS spies infiltrate almost every one of the scores of parallel sessions conducted at the congress. They scout for new ideas from others, then go home to IRS headquarters and try to implement what they have learned by scavenging. And guess who pays for their expensive trips, meals and lodging.

Most statisticians are honest, hard-working professionals. They naturally resent the blatant theft of their ideas by someone out to get them and the rest of us. Consequently, people attending the conferences tend not to talk to the dozens of IRS personnel buzzing around, considering them a nuisance. At one meeting, the session chair introduced the speaker from the IRS and joked: "She'll be taking your names and social security numbers, so don't leave the

THE IRS
STATISTICIAN IS
EVER LOOKING
TO IMPROVE THE
DIF

room...." Typically, when an IRS paper is presented, many other statisticians will leave the room. Those who stay will almost always keep quiet and not ask questions or offer suggestions. The IRS personnel in each meeting room will often circulate, aggressively asking others for advice on how to solve their statistical problems.

At one such meeting in San Francisco, an IRS statistician was presenting a paper: "Who Are the Nonfilers, and How Can We Catch Them?" The paper, presented at a session that otherwise had interesting presentations by academics and industrial statisticians, stuck out like a sore thumb. It said nothing and consisted of a few transparent statements that all led to the same question: How can we, the IRS, use statistics to catch nonfilers? Here is a short excerpt (reprinted in *SOI Bulletin*, Summer 1993, p.55):

> ...SOI's ability to profile prior-year returns is based entirely on their being filed, processed and subject to sampling. In essence, SOI can only analyze "what comes in;" hence, it is necessary to note that SOI *cannot* measure the universe of "unknown" nonfilers *not in the system*. SOI can capture data on "unknown" nonfilers only *after* they file.

(Quotation marks and italics are all theirs.) The paper was part of the IRS's program called *Compliance 2000*, the purpose of which is to use statistics to "remove barriers to compliance" by the year 2000....

Then the presenter invited a "discussion" from the audience. Many people were offended and left the room in disgust, some making snide comments. Of those who remained, no one uttered a word. Finally one person raised his hand. With a thick British accent he went on to explain how the Inland Revenue Office in the U.K. catches nonfilers. The six IRS statisticians attending the session as well as the presenter all got out their notepads and feverishly started writing down everything that was said....

Generally less qualified and lower-paid than others, SOI statisticians need to continuously improve that dinosaur of a DIF and their other statistical implements, to make them more efficient for more and more audit-driven tax revenues. From the government's point of view, paying for these annual trips to conferences is a cheap way of trying to do the trick. But they get exactly what they pay for. In fact, another article in the same issue of the *SOI Bulletin* referred to above admits:

> Many government statistical agencies, including SOI, have not kept up with the explosive growth of statistical theory and methods.

It was at one such annual statistical meeting that the idea first germinated in my brain: statistics can be used both ways—by the government *and* by the taxpayer! I decided to use my own knowledge of statistics, which I believe to be far superior to that of the IRS statisticians, to do battle with them. I would use all the advanced methods at my disposal to defeat the DIF. I will do so by using statistics to estimate the actual DIF, and I will give you the results.

But before we get to my statistical remedy for audit—the

statistical armor I am going to give you—I want you to know some things about the audit process itself. This will motivate you to do everything you can to avoid this experience and to work toward keeping as much of your hard-earned dollars from the taxman while minimizing the chance of an audit.

CHAPTER 6

AN ADVERSARIAL
RELATIONSHIP

A TAX AUDIT IS
AN IRS GAME
AIMED AT
DEFEATING YOU

T he most important thing for you to remember when dealing with IRS agents is that they are *not* your friends, no matter what. By the very nature of the system, the IRS is out to get you. The IRS is a greedy bureaucracy with the sole purpose of sucking money out of us like a huge vacuum cleaner. Horror stories have surfaced from time to time about checks made out to third parties arriving by mistake at IRS processing centers and being altered and cashed by the agency, leaving their proper owners to sue for reimbursement.

The IRS game is a *zero-sum* game. This means that only one party to the game can win. This is a battle for every single dollar. The IRS spends tremendous amounts of resources trying to extract as much as possible from all of us. Laws are constantly being written to make it very difficult for you to shield your income from taxation. And it gets worse every year. The Alternative Minimum Tax (AMT) is a good example of this. The AMT was designed not long ago for the sole purpose of making it impossible for you to use your deductions effectively. As soon as you can reduce your tax by any significant amount, that convoluted trap called AMT kicks in and wipes out much of your tax reduction.

The IRS will always interpret laws in its favor. The tax law consists of thousands of pages of legislation, rulings, and precedents. It is designed to be fair to the taxpayer, but interpretations can vary widely. So even if the law will give you a break on a particular item, it does not mean that the IRS will. Once the IRS agent looks at the particular issue in question, he or she will interpret the law in favor of the IRS. Often, there are IRS guidelines on how to handle various issues. Then, as a result of litigation, courts make provisions and interpret the law in a way that allows the taxpayer some latitude. In most cases, the auditor, who is usually a relatively low-level IRS employee, will *not* be aware of the court ruling that allows you to make use of some deduction to your advantage. At the audit, you will be left having to fight for your right to the deduction with a person who does not know the ruling and is not willing to allow you a wider interpretation. "I read this rule to mean that I don't have to capitalize these expenses over four years" may not convince the auditor who believes that you had to capitalize and therefore were entitled to a much smaller tax deduction for that year. You will have to find the particular statute or precedent allowing you to do what you did when you prepared your return. At the audit, fighting for your rights against a stubborn adversary who is not well-versed in the subtleties of the tax law is an uphill battle.

THE IRS WILL ALWAYS INTERPRET THE LAW IN THE WORST POSSIBLE WAY FOR YOU

The audit process is a thorough investigation of every declared item. If there is any way at all that an issue can be interpreted in a way that leads to more dollars for the government, the agent will do so. At the end of the audit, the agent will give you his or her report including all the disallowances of your deductions that the agent believes result from the audit. Then you will have to fight for your rights first with the agent, then with his or her supervisor, an appeals officer, and possibly in court.

IRS agents are soldiers in an army designed for the purpose of getting your dollars. The agents are trained extensively for that purpose: while they usually do not see the entire IRS picture, they are programmed to perform a series of tasks aimed at getting more money from you. At the audit you are in the hands of an inquisitor out to get you to confess to cheating the government. Disallowing your deductions is one step; finding your unreported income is the final goal.

NEVER TRUST AN IRS AGENT

Do not be fooled by social graces or small talk or niceties. The IRS agent is not your friend. He or she is only interested in one thing: your money. Hang tight and don't give an inch. The agent is *trained* in psychological methods that are designed to intimidate you. The IRS manuals contain explicit instructions to their agents on how to make you uncomfortable, how to exert psychological pressure on you, and how to intimidate you. Everything is so by design. Nothing is casual even if it may seem so.

The agent will call you at home, often at inconvenient times such as 7 AM or worse. The agent will call you at work, exposing you to your employer or co-workers as someone who is being "audited by the IRS." The agent will meet you in his/her territory, where you will sit in a dark and stuffy room waiting for the agent to ask questions, demand explanations.

All of this is designed so that you will feel pushed and uncomfortable and will do exactly what the IRS agent wants you to do: admit that your claims and deductions were unreasonable. Maybe you will even reveal that hidden income they are after, and as a bonus give them that foreign bank account they know you have...and under threat of a criminal investigation you will agree to pay a lot more tax and interest and penalties and the agent will look good in the eyes of supervisors and will eventually be promoted.

But also remember that the IRS agent is still (hard to admit) human. As such, the agent has weaknesses just like you and me. The trick is, of course, to find those weaknesses and exploit them to *your* advantage. The auditor is trying to make an assessment: is this an honest person, or one who has hidden some income which I can find? The way to behave in such an encounter is to try to gain the agent's confidence.

This can be done by various methods, and is a tricky task. One tax attorney I know has an interesting habit. He tries to look over the auditor's shoulder at his or her calendar. If the calendar looks full, the agent is very busy and then one strategy will be used by the attorney: delay, be indirect, stretch things out.

One tactic that seems to work is to ask a lot of questions:

35

Why do you need this? What should I do in this situation? I thought this was a reasonable way to handle this issue, don't you? Etc. This tends to throw off the auditor. He or she may also get tired of answering your questions and will want to get the examination over with.

Some IRS agents, especially the young, tend to be idealistic in some bizarre way: they believe that their mission is to *educate* you, the taxpayer. They want to teach you how to do your taxes correctly so that you will not be audited in the future (as if incorrect filing is what got you to them in the first place!). These auditors are easier to handle because they have a clear weakness. Here you should cater to the agent's desire to educate you. Ask questions on how you could do your taxes better. "How can I learn from this experience so that next time I will not be audited?" or "I want to learn to prepare my taxes well," etc. You will be surprised how far such an approach can get you with an agent bent on a mission of "educating" you about the tax system. Defer to such an agent and he or she may even forget what they are there for—if you're lucky.

CHAPTER 7

NEVER PANIC!

So you got that letter calling you for an audit by the IRS. The worst thing you can do is to panic. Take some time to think. Do not act quickly. In fact, this is probably the best advice I can give you. Time is always on your side, *even though* time will cost you interest if you have been determined to owe the government more tax. The IRS is under very tight time constraints. This fact cannot be over-emphasized. The audit process begins right after you file, when returns are entered into the big IRS computer in West Virginia. The DIF starts to work immediately, spewing out the identification codes for those returns that need to be audited.

THE TIME ELEMENT:

THE IRS HAS THREE YEARS FROM THE TIME YOUR
RETURN IS DUE (USUALLY APRIL 15) TO ASK FOR
MORE TAX

We need to mention some exceptions. If the IRS determines that you have not declared 25% or more of your income, they have six years to complete your audit. Also, if you are a nonfiler, then since there was no date of filing, they have no date for completing your investigation! They can take forever. The time line of the audit game is shown in Figure 1.

FIGURE 1.

The time line of the audit game

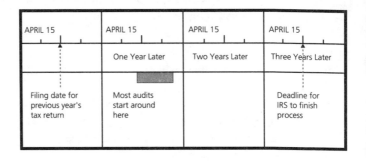

This means that if you filed your 1994 return on April 15, 1995, the government must finish the audit by April 15, 1998 if they want to ask for additional tax. This may *seem* like a very long period of time. In effect, it is quite short. Anyone experienced in the incredibly inefficient bureaucracy of the U.S. government will recognize this fact. While a proficient private accountant could complete an audit of your entire tax return in a single afternoon, you would be surprised that the same return can take an IRS agent 6 months, a year, or even more to conclude! A recent IRS publication on "Taxpayer Burden in the IRS" states that the *average* elapsed time in examination in 1990 was 44 weeks. Strange that they would even admit in an official publication how incredibly inefficient they are. There are many reasons for this unfathomable inefficiency. First of all, the IRS agent is not as qualified, nor as motivated as a private accountant. And IRS agents are typically very overworked. They are 9-to-5 types who have to conduct a certain number of audits in a given period of time. They sit in their offices and then go home. They have no incentive to do a good job, to work overtime, or to be efficient at what they do.

While the IRS system is itself computerized, the agents are not. An experiment in training the agents in the use of personal computers a few years ago was declared a complete failure. The agents remain pencil-and-paper people, who take their time looking at your file, misplacing it, working on another file for a while, going on to yet a third file, calling in sick, and attending training meetings. If you are lucky, they may even lose your file or misplace it for an extended period of time and pass their deadline of three years from the time you filed, and you are then home free. Even the most efficient and dedicated agent may take several months to complete an audit of your return. If they make a mistake, if they are stalled long enough, if they lose your file—you gain from it, and may be off the hook completely.

There is another, rather touchy point about time. Audits are usually initiated 14 to 17 months after you have filed your return. If the audit is taking longer than the agent

IRS AGENTS ARE TYPICALLY OVERWORKED AND PRESSED FOR TIME. USE THIS FACT TO YOUR ADVANTAGE: DELAY!

REMEMBER, TIME IS ON YOUR SIDE: WELCOME ANY DELAY AND LOOK FOR ANY EXCUSE TO ASK FOR POSTPONEMENTS

39

expected, and the deadline—three years from the filing date—is approaching, the IRS may request that you sign an extension consent form. Usually, the requested extension is for six more months beyond the deadline (Form 872), although the IRS may request that you sign an indefinite extension (Form 872-A). What happens here is that the IRS admits that they have been slow and inefficient in conducting the audit of your return and that all the time they had (three years from the time you filed!) was still not enough for them and therefore they now want *you* to give up your constitutional right to have this horrendous process over within a reasonable time. Personally, I never give up my rights, and I don't think that you should, either. Congress enacts laws for the good of our society. While the laws should be fair to the taxpayer, most of the tax law system favors the IRS and is designed to increase government revenues. Few laws are there to protect the citizen from abuse by the all-powerful IRS. The law limiting the time the IRS has to collect money from you is, therefore, almost an exception. It is a small provision designed to protect you from being harassed forever by the agency.

There is a trick, however, that allows the IRS to abuse its powers against you and to help them *make* you give up your right to end the process—in case you haven't guessed. The IRS will use the following reasoning to pressure you to sign away your rights: We need more time to check your claims and deductions, so that we can allow them to stand. As they are right now, we will have to *disallow* them. If you give us the time we need by signing the extension form, we will use the time for this purpose. If you don't sign, we will disallow all deductions that we had no time to check. This incredibly warped logic is consistent, however, with the IRS being all-powerful and your having no defense against them. It sits well with the assumption that you are guilty until *you* prove you are innocent. This practice amounts to official blackmail. The IRS uses it daily. If this happens to you, you will have to make a difficult choice. Sometimes delaying the decision itself as to whether or not to sign the extension may get you over the problem, because in the meantime the deadline will have slipped by. In such a case, you win everything—there will be no assessment. But more often, the IRS agent will be aware of the need to have the extension form signed before the deadline arrives and will pressure you to sign. As a rule, you should never sign the *indefinite* extension form, Form 872-A. If the auditor asks you to sign it, argue that you do not see why he or she would need an indefinite extension, and that one for six more months should be more than enough (Form 872).

Usually, the auditor will ask you to sign the limited extension form (872). However, you should try your best not to sign the limited extension either. It often happens that once you sign Form 872, the audit will continue and eventually the inefficient snail-paced auditor will again ask you to sign the extension form for another six months.... Once you are dragged into the cycle of giving up your rights to allow the excesses of the IRS to continue, you may be a lost soul, forever audited. Such extended audits can last for years! The best tactic is to be evasive. Outright *refusal* to sign the form may not be in your best interest. The auditor may simply make good on the threat and assess you in the worst possible way—this is your punishment for

THE IRS WILL TRY
TO PUSH YOU
TO GIVE UP
YOUR RIGHT TO
HAVE THE AUDIT
FINISHED WITH-
IN THE LEGAL
TIME LIMIT.RESIST
THE PRESSURE!

not signing away your rights. You could still appeal, but you will be one step behind in this difficult game. As is the case in most situations dealing with the IRS, indirect, evasive strategies are the best.

So in any case (leaving out the fact that interest may be accruing), time is on your side. Take your time. If the letter gives you 30 days to respond to the audit request, take 30 days. Use the time to work out a strategy. Look over all your records and compile the information the IRS has requested. Obtain copies of missing records, such as misplaced bank statements, etc.

In addition to the time element, the *information* element works on your side. The IRS agent is on a fishing expedition. Because of the priorities of the IRS, the first being the chase for unreported income, the agent conducting the investigation will be looking hard to find any missing income. The agent often has no idea where to look or what to look for. He or she got your return because the computer tagged it, but often has no clue as to why this happened.

THE IRS
AUDIT IS A
COMPREHENSIVE
SEARCH FOR
INFORMATION:
EVIDENCE THAT
YOU UNDERPAID
YOUR TAX

The agent follows the IRS priorities: first look for any hidden income; second, look for deductions that cannot be fully substantiated. So don't help the IRS do its work. Give an agent no information unless he or she asks for it. Be as tight-lipped as you possibly can. It is a crime punishable by law to lie to the IRS. However, evasive answers such as "I will get back to you on this later," are not a crime. Delay, take your time, think, give no additional information.

A third element on your side—and most definitely the most important one—is your brain. If you bought this book, chances are you are much more intelligent than your typical IRS agent. Use your brain! You are engaged in a battle for your dollars against a stubborn, vicious adversary. Take your time, compose yourself, and try to answer as little as possible. Time is on your side, you control much of the information the IRS receives, and you can use your wits in the battle against them. If you play your hand well, you may win the IRS audit game.

NEVER GIVE THE IRS AGENT ANY INFORMATION HE OR SHE HAS NOT ASKED FOR.

In case you are suspected of criminal tax evasion or criminal nonfiling of returns, the above advice is even more important. The IRS agents are trained in *entrapping* you. In many ways, they operate outside the law. They will give you no Miranda rights, and will ask you "Catch 22" questions that will entrap you either way you answer. For example, if you did not file a tax return and the agent asks you: "Did you file your tax return for 1994?" you lose any way you answer. If you answer: "No," you just admitted to the crime of non-filing. If you answer "Yes," when in fact you did not file, you just lied to the IRS, which is an even worse crime. Both are punishable by law and may result in prison terms. The only right answer in this case is no answer at all, something like: "I will get back to you after I consult my accountant (attorney)."

BEWARE OF THE IRS TRYING TO ENTRAP YOU: BE CAREFUL ANSWERING QUESTIONS

Panic may take different forms. Some people freak out when they get The Letter. To avoid having to go through the terrifying experience themselves (and often also feeling their time is too valuable to be wasted in an audit) these people hire a tax lawyer or accountant to go in for them.

This may be a big mistake. Assuming you prepared your own return, no one else knows your tax situation as well as you do. No one else can explain certain expenses, deductions, losses, credits the way you can. Trust someone else to do the job and indeed you will not have to face the IRS agent. But on the other hand, in addition to having to pay high attorney or accountant fees, you may also have to pay more taxes as a result of the audit than you would have to pay if you faced the enemy yourself. Additionally, tax attorneys and tax accountants are agents hired on your behalf. However, your best interest may not always be *their* best interest. These professionals deal with the IRS on a daily basis. They have a strong incentive not to burn any bridges, not to antagonize anyone, and to maintain friendly relations with IRS personnel. For the sake of a future relationship with the IRS, your hired agent may be willing to sacrifice some of your interests now.

There are, of course, situations where you may need a tax professional. You also need to understand the difference between the two types of tax professionals: attorneys, and accountants. An attorney may not be as well versed in accounting, but should know the law better than an accountant, so if you are in *serious* trouble with the IRS, for example, if you are under investigation by the Criminal Investigations Division (CID), you probably need an attorney. Attorneys are bound by attorney-client privilege, which means that if they find that you did something wrong they may not be forced to reveal such "privileged" information to the IRS, or to anyone. If you have a *serious* accounting problem with your return, without legal complications, you may need to hire an accountant to help

BE AWARE THAT YOUR BEST INTEREST AND THAT OF THE TAX PROFESSIONAL REPRESENTING YOU MAY NOT ALWAYS COINCIDE

your case with the IRS. Accountants, however, are not bound by the injunction against revealing "privileged" client information.

In general, unless there are unusual complications, you are usually better off going alone with the IRS. You are always your best advocate. You know your circumstances, and only you can find more receipts and substantiations after the audit has begun. A tax professional representing you may simply look in the file and say "No, we have no receipts," thus losing you a point that will cost you money. Going it alone gives you more possibilities, more time, and more maneuverability in this nasty game. A tax professional may simply not be willing to take quite as many chances or gambles in the audit process, and thus weaken your case significantly.

Then there is another, rather delicate point. A large percentage of the IRS auditors are young, and often attractive, women. On the other hand, many tax professionals, lawyers and accountants, tend to be middle-aged men. I believe that the IRS is quite aware of this fact, and that they hire young women by design, not so much because they believe in equal opportunity for women but rather for other reasons. First, because the workplace in our society is still sexist, women agree to work at lower pay than men. Since the IRS, as a government agency, cannot offer very high pay, it fills many positions with women. Younger women, with less experience, work for even lower pay. The second reason, I believe, is that the IRS wants to have young women as auditors. When dealing with a tax professional representing an audited taxpayer—and sometimes when dealing directly with the taxpayer—a young woman may be able to get the upper hand against an older man. This does not have to be in the tangible way seen in at least one recent TV movie, where the audited police detective agrees to all the assessments against him in the hope that after the audit the attractive young IRS auditor will go out with him. It can take subtler forms, which are no less effective. At least one tax attorney, when confronted with having done a poor job for his client, finally admitted: "She was really cute... I don't know...the disallowances she made seemed quite reasonable to me.... Anyway, you didn't lose much, and she needs a break if she wants to climb up the IRS ladder." This type of thing happens a lot more often than you think.

You don't need anyone to protect you—they may not protect you at all. Bide your time, look for any possible delay, be composed, and when you need time to produce a record—ask for it. The IRS cannot deny you the right to have ample time to present your case in the best possible way. As you go along, you can always consult with a tax professional on the more difficult issues, *without* giving up control of your case to someone else. Only you can do this best—if you don't panic.

CHAPTER 8

DAMAGE CONTROL

S o you didn't panic, you took your time to answer the letter, and you came to your meeting with the agent. What next? The amount of hassle and damage you receive in the audit process depends on many factors—but the most important one is you. At least one person has committed suicide following an endless audit. He simply could not take the harassment any longer. His son, who was supposed to receive a small refund from the IRS, got a letter from the agency instead, telling him that his refund was applied toward paying some of the tax owed by his deceased father! The truth is that even death will not end your audit. If you die, your executors will have to continue with the audit. You need to remember, however, that you are dealing with a huge and inefficient bureaucracy. Some people have found that moving to a new state, or telling the IRS they will be overseas for a period of time after the IRS requests the audit, has gotten them off the hook. When files are transferred to another location, or when delays are forced on the Service, files may fall through the cracks and the target of the audit goes free.

ANYTHING
UNUSUAL THAT
MAY HAPPEN
WITH YOUR FILE
COULD GET
YOU OFF

If this does not happen to you, tough it out. Taking a tough, if civil and polite stance against the IRS is probably your best defense. Asking questions may help diffuse the attack against you as well. Try to find out from the agent anything you can about your case. Why is your return being examined? Once you find out—if you do—try to *limit* the agent's investigation to only that item. Be pushy: If this item is under question, here is the proof you need, now let's get it over with! Of course this approach may not always work, but it is definitely worth the chance. Remember that whatever got your file questioned is only the hook to get someone who looks—statistically—like a person who may lead the government to more money: hidden income treasures, overinflated deductions, who knows....

DO EVERYTHING
YOU CAN TO
TRY TO LIMIT THE
SCOPE OF THE
AUDIT

The IRS agent may want to continue looking at *other* categories which may lead to the treasures. Effective damage control will be your ability to limit the investigation as much as possible. What may work in your favor, as in any situation of conflict—are the weaknesses of the enemy. Agents are overworked, pressed for time, limited in their ability, and—most of all—lazy. One trick that often works is to do the agent's homework for him or her. For example, suppose that you forgot a small item you should have declared on your return—an IRA you cashed without reporting and paying the penalty. Do the homework for the agent, do the correction in perfect accounting form, admit the small additional amount you owe and ask the agent to finish the audit. This face-saving item you gave the auditor, resulting in a small gain for the government, may lead to the case being closed (and possibly costing you much less than if a more thorough investigation were to result). You should never, however, concede large items. The agent may never find them; the investigation may lead in other directions, away from the large errors.

IRS agents have access to an incredible array of information about you. Some of the information may be obtained directly from you, other facts from different sources. It is hard to describe just how much someone can learn about you by looking at your canceled checks: virtually everything about your life is there. In an audit, your boxes of canceled checks—copies of which the IRS can get from your financial institutions if you cannot find all the checks—could be carefully scrutinized. This does not happen in every audit, but it happens whenever the agent decides that an in-depth examination is warranted or when there is a suspicion of hidden income.

Not only will the amounts of your checks be totalled and compared with the deposits to look *directly* for hidden income, but the names of the payees will be scrutinized. The agent will also look for any signs of alteration. Look at your own checks now and ask yourself: Is there anything here that will arouse an auditor's suspicion? Any transfer of funds, and especially foreign exchange will get you very close attention. In looking for hidden income, the agent can speak to other people who may have knowledge of your lifestyle, as well as obtain other documents directly from you. If you keep a foreign bank account, indirect methods such as looking at your passport can be used by the IRS to determine frequent trips to offshore destinations known to have non-reporting foreign banks.

NEVER BRING TO THE AUDIT ANYTHING OTHER THAN THE ITEMS ASKED FOR

YOUR CANCELED CHECKS TELL THE IRS THE STORY OF YOUR LIFE

Then a more direct inquiry can nail the actual bank account with your hidden income.

Large cash transactions can also tip off the agent. The IRS is well aware that cash, because it is fluid and generally non-traceable, is a good way to hide your transactions. This is one reason why institutions are required to report to the government all cash transactions of $10,000 or more. If you make purchases or transfers of large amounts, records of these transactions may be obtained by the IRS. The agent is then well on the way to finding hidden income.

The IRS has incredible computer power for searching for information on the taxpayer. A computer information system called TECS (Treasury Enforcement Communication System) is a major tool that can be tapped by an agent looking for information on you. Any information the Department of the Treasury may have collected on a taxpayer is coded in TECS. This includes information from the Customs Service on any expensive goods imported from abroad, and any other information Treasury may collect.

Recently, IRS personnel started downloading computer files from a wide variety of sources to workstations and personal computers, where segments of the databases may be separately analyzed in search of information on hidden income sources. The databases used are lists of business transactions of all kinds, memberships in organizations, subscriptions of all kinds, deeds and real estate records, licensing data and more. This approach uses what might be called the chain-letter principle and is similar to the system that gets your name on ever more mailing lists even against your will and without your knowledge. Powerful computers search for your name and social security number in an ever-increasing number of databases that are available to the IRS.

The twin powers of parallel processing and modern computer network design make the IRS ever more efficient in searching for information on any taxpayer. The tremendous advances that are taking place in this technology help the IRS invade your privacy. Big Brother is using computers to spy on your every move. This invasion is bound to get *much* worse in the near future. Be extremely careful with the information you give the IRS. Never give more than they ask for.

THE "INFORMATION SUPERHIGHWAY" IS A GREAT FRIEND TO THE IRS

CHAPTER 9

THE LET'S-MAKE-A-DEAL TRAP

W ithout looking at all your records and receipts, the agent might suddenly say: "I'll accept half your deductions." This is not a casual remark. It is the result of intensive training the IRS gives its agents. It is part of a new effort the IRS is making in reducing the resources that go into tax investigations; it wants maximum revenue at minimum effort. Often, when the assessment of additional tax is made and a taxpayer appeals or goes to court, half the new assessments are thrown out. The new approach, which allows half of everything right away, may minimize the effort on the part of the government. The IRS hates appeals, and more than anything, it hates going to court. If you will agree to a fifty-fifty settlement right away, the agency can avoid a lot of effort.

This approach by the IRS, however, is a despicable trap. First, it assumes that you lied about everything. And now the IRS will do you this big favor of "forgiving" half your debt. Even if you really lied, this deal is no bed of roses. If you accept this gambit, you will not gain anything! Yes, the IRS will accept half your claims and make you pay for the other half. But, and here comes the big "but"—first of

BEWARE OF AN OFFER BY THE AGENT TO ACCEPT HALF YOUR CLAIMS WITHOUT LOOKING AT ANYTHING

all, you will have to pay penalties and interest, and these alone may get you closer to the half you thought you were getting away with. Secondly, an important point indeed: the IRS now has caught you. You have just admitted—indirectly—that you lied about your return, and they will get you many, many ways. Your DIF score will rise dramatically. This means that in the future you will be audited again and again.

SETTLING FOR LESS THAN YOU DESERVE MAY ALSO CONDEMN YOU TO FUTURE AUDITS

As we will discuss next, the audit is not over when one year has been examined. The IRS can now look at more years, come back later and audit other years. You will never get out of the hole once you take this bait. Even if you lied about everything, you should never accept a fifty-fifty offer from the IRS. Let them look at every item, while you fight them for it. Give them a run for their money. Make it difficult and lengthy and costly for them to get anything from you. You gain nothing by accepting such an offer.

The worst of it is, of course, when the taxpayer is honest, pays the government its due and then gets caught in an audit because statistically people in his or her category tend to be picked up by the DIF. Here is a person with legitimate claims and deductions, with receipts for everything, but with limited time to go through an all-consuming audit that can drag on for months and wear out even the toughest among us. The IRS, experts in terrorizing and intimidating, make you this tempting offer. I will accept half and you don't have to show me receipts or substantiation for *anything*. Just sign here. The government is all-powerful. It can legally try to make the most outrageous deals with you. Just say no! Let the IRS agent sweat it out. Fight him or her on every single point. Then, when the tax examination is over—then may be the time to make deals. Make deals when *you* are ahead. Why? Once the examination is over, the IRS agent will make an assessment. This will include all the new taxes the agent believes you owe because you lacked substantiation for the deductions you claimed. And, if the agent believes there is evidence of unreported income, this will also be added into the assessment. You will now have the choice of either agreeing with the assessment and paying the additional tax and penalties and interest, or appealing to a higher level. It is almost never a good idea to agree. You should always appeal, unless the result of the audit is so much in your favor that there is nothing to appeal—you are getting money back.

DON'T LET THE AGENT PUSH YOU TO SETTLE, GIVING UP YOUR RIGHT TO AN APPEAL

Once you inform the agent of your intention to appeal the assessment, the agent will have a strong incentive to make a deal with you—a deal that will be much more in your favor than the deal offered initially. This may be a deal on your terms. The reason for this is quite simple: no IRS agent wants to have his or her work appealed, gone over by a supervisor, scrutinized, possibly criticized by a higher-ranking IRS official. This does not look good for the agent, who will seem weak and ineffective. At this point, if the agent sees that you intend to appeal, a favorable offer may be made to you. Think about it. You may still want to appeal. And the offers can get better and better as time goes on. If you appeal and lose, and if your case is strong enough, you may then go to tax court. Tax court usually will not require an attorney, unless your case is

Chapter 9

54

complicated or the amounts are large. The court is designed as a People's Court. You present your case and so does the Service, and the judge will make a decision. Going to court, however, is costly to the government. If you show your intention to go to court, a more favorable offer to settle out of court may be made to you.

CHAPTER 10

THE HUNT FOR HIDDEN TREASURE

Your first meeting with the IRS agent is an important one. Remember that you don't want to give the agent any information. Information, however, is conveyed also by indirect means. IRS agents are trained at making judgements about your likely actual income based on your lifestyle. They scrutinize how you look: do you wear expensive clothing or jewelry? This may imply a higher standard of living that your reported income would allow. Do you drive a more expensive car than your reported income could support? Leave your Porsche at home...preferably take public transportation to the interview. An IRS interview is one place you *don't* want to impress anyone with how much money you have. When making small talk with the agent, talk about the weather. Don't talk about your experience cruising the Caribbean, and it's probably not a good idea to discuss politics. About the last thing an IRS agent wants to hear from you is complaints about how your tax dollars are spent.

NEVER GIVE THE
IRS AGENT THE
IMPRESSION
THAT YOU HAVE
MONEY

The IRS agent will look at the face of the return and try to get a feel for whether or not the reported income makes sense given your perceived lifestyle. IRS agents are accountants, low-level ones for the most part, but accountants nonetheless. The agent thinks like an accountant when searching for that hidden income—the number one priority in the audit. Therefore, you need to understand the accounting principle that underlies the treasure hunt.

The treasure-hunting accounting principle:

$$INCOME = EXPENDITURES + SAVINGS$$

Or, in simple English: What goes in must come out. The IRS agent will try to balance your books to his or her satisfaction. The theory is that once everything that goes in has been identified, and everything that comes out has been accounted for as well, the true level of your income will magically emerge.

This approach is—at best—naive. To see that, just ask yourself if *you* could do such a balancing act with your own bank books. Once you have been netted in the IRS audit net, the agent will likely ask to see your bank statements and try to match all deposit amounts with all checks written. Look back at your bank books and see whether you can match the amounts. If you are like most people, you don't have a record of every check written years ago. And what was that $1,500 deposit? I can't remember now. What you cannot remember, the agent will write down as "unsubstantiated" and will explicitly assume it was *income*. Remember that the burden of proof in an audit is on you and not on the IRS—here, you are assumed *guilty* until *you* prove your innocence. Try to find—before any audit—a substantiation for every possible item: deposit, check, expense, credit-card charge. Leave nothing to chance or the enemy will use it to hang you. A substantiation—both in the case of the nebulous hidden income and in the case of deductions of various kinds—does not have to be of perfect quality, but it must be there. A word to the wise.

THE IRS CAN USE *INDIRECT* METHODS TO PROVE YOU HAVE HIDDEN INCOME

Another favorite method of the IRS in finding unreported income is the Net Worth method. Here the auditor computes what he or she believes is your net worth in the beginning of the year and at the end of the year. Your net worth is the sum of the values of all your assets, including all amounts in cash at banks and other financial institutions, *minus* all your liabilities (your debts, including your mortgage and other loans). Any increase in your net worth over the year will then be checked. If the total increase in your net worth cannot be explained by your reported income as well as other reported sources such as capital gains or gain in property value, the remainder will be attributed to unreported income. This is an *indirect* method of looking for unreported income. The balance-your-books method is direct because it looks at every visible transaction: deposits, checks, etc. The Net Worth method looks for the total accumulation in the entire year. This method, too, has pitfalls and ample opportunity for errors and abuse by the IRS. As part of this tack of the investigation, the auditor may ask you to fill out Form 4822, listing your living expenses for the year. Most people grossly underestimate their living expenses, thus giving the IRS the noose with which to hang them. If you underestimate your living expenses, this will overestimate the amount left over and that, in turn, will be interpreted as the result of some hidden income!

NEVER AGREE TO GIVE THE AUDITOR A LISTING OF YOUR LIVING EXPENSES

What makes the search for hidden treasures so preposterous is the fact that people who truly hide income are immune to this kind of matching search. The innocent and the careless are the ones who have unexplained items when the books are balanced in the hands of the IRS. That $1,500 was probably a birthday gift from your mother, or a reimbursed business expense, or maybe you deposited travelers checks left over from the previous summer's trip to Europe. Truly hidden income would never be casually deposited in a bank, where it can be so easily traced. But go try to argue that with the IRS. And the amounts can grow extremely fast. A few items such as these on the deposit side and a few missing checks on the outlay side and the agent will conclude that you had $20,000 in additional, unreported income. Errors will easily compound and affect your computed net worth change for the year as well—leading to the assumption you have some additional income that you did not report.

That person who does have $20,000 in unreported income very likely laughs at the silly IRS accountants—his or her books will very neatly balance at the lower, reported amount of income claimed of the tax return. The unreported income most probably was in cash, and it did not go into any bank account, neither did it go toward the purchase of a large item that can be traced and show an increase in net worth. And if it did, it wasn't a bank account or a property in this country, so it is not declared anywhere or reported to the IRS. Hiding income can be relatively easy for the person who realizes how the IRS looks for such hidden treasures—by balancing the visible "in" with the visible "out" or by looking for an increase in visible wealth. The honest person needs to protect himself or herself from false accusations of having hidden income.

It is worth noting that many credit card companies now allow their customers to write checks against their credit account, and the amounts are then billed on the customer's usual monthly statement. Such charges, payable to any third party exactly like bank checks, are—at this writing—not reported as bank transactions. You are not sent the canceled check, nor does your statement show who was paid, or a check number. Such transfers of funds may not be visible to the IRS agent conducting an audit.

Again, be careful with the impression you give of yourself to the Service, and understand that there is more to the process than simple book balancing. If your records show large amounts expended on luxury items that the agent suspects are above your means, this could lead to much closer scrutiny even if your books balance. The last thing you want to do is to arouse suspicion. Remember that the IRS has virtually unlimited powers against you. If the agent suspects you of having a larger income to support the expenses he or she believes that you have, the investigation could expand, and you will be faced with having to prove a lot more. You want to be cautious and anticipate problems before you are faced with an audit. Write down a short note of explanation next to every large or unusual bank deposit or check written. Do your best to appear to live a notch lower than your actual standard of living. This way you will be sure to remain beyond suspicion of having unreported income.

CHAPTER 11

THE MULTI-YEAR CANCER

An IRS audit is a cancer. Like all malignant tumors, it starts small: a little letter, somewhat individualized by handwriting, asking for specific items to be examined. Once you contract the disease, it spreads and spreads. It starts with one year, then the agent asks you to see the returns for other years. What most people do not realize about the IRS is that an audit is rarely for one particular tax year only. The initial year is audited because the computer decided that you look like the people who owe more tax. Then the logic goes: if this person owes more tax (even *before* this assessment is made!), then let's see what we can get for *other* tax years as well! It is important to understand that any tax year may be audited as long as three years have not elapsed since a tax return was filed for that year.

Laws are somewhat ambiguous about when an additional year may be audited, and therefore the IRS agent will typically be sneaky. But make no mistake, the agent's supervisor *strongly* encourages the agent to audit other tax years as well as the one currently being examined. Often, the agent will say, while auditing your 1993 return: "Have you filed for 1994 yet? I would like to look at your file to see how you handled this item in 1994, for comparison." If you give the agent your 1994 return, you have just helped the agent start another audit!

The best technique is to be evasive. Tell the agent you will "look for it at home," and then say nothing about it the next time you meet with him or her. Hopefully the investigator, overworked and eager to finish, will have forgotten or given up on it. Legally, you may ignore such requests as long as they are not in *writing*. If the IRS agent requests in writing to see other years, you must submit the returns.

THE IRS WILL TRY
TO EXPAND THE
AUDIT TO
INCLUDE AS
MANY OTHER
TAX YEARS AS
POSSIBLE

Which years may be audited by the IRS? Any tax return that has been filed by the time of the audit and for which the three-year time limit on audits has not yet expired is called an "open" year. The IRS has the right to audit any open year. For example, suppose that you always file your return on April 15th, when it is due. On April 15th of 1992 you filed your 1991 tax return; on April 15, 1993, you filed for 1992; and on April 15, 1994 you filed your 1993 return. Now suppose that in March 1995 you are audited for tax year 1992. Since three years have not yet elapsed since April 1992, tax year 1991 is still *open*. The agent can therefore also audit your 1991 return. The year 1990 is no longer open since the time limit for that tax year was exceeded on April 15, 1994. Now comes a very important point. If your audit continues past April 15th of 1995, what should you do? Do not file your 1994 return! If you do file, the IRS agent can now audit that year as well—as it will have just become "open." Ask for an automatic extension to file your tax return late (by August 15). If your audit is still not over by early August, ask for a second extension, which the IRS will grant if you have a good reason, allowing you to file by October 15. Hopefully, your case will then be over.

NEVER FILE A TAX RETURN WHILE AN AUDIT IS IN PROGRESS

The wisdom of this advice has even been admitted by an IRS agent who said to me: "Don't tell my boss I told you this, but no one should ever file while being audited." While you are being audited, the IRS agent will bring up your record on the computer. The computer is programmed to automatically show all open years. The built-in calendar immediately adjusts to show which years have been filed, which can no longer be audited, and which are now open. This makes it quite easy for the IRS to actually conduct audits of as many years as possible for any given person. Auditing more years for a person suspected initially of hiding income or over-claiming deductions can be a profitable undertaking for the government. It requires no new resources—it uses the same person who is auditing for the year in question. And such expanded audits have a good chance for added revenue.

USE ANY EXCUSE YOU CAN TO KEEP THE AGENT AWAY FROM YOUR OTHER OPEN YEARS

Of course this system is absurd, as it can result in an "endless" audit for the unlucky person caught in this web. If you *do* file your returns when they are due while an audit is in progress—for example, you file for 1994 on April 15, 1995, while your audit for 1992 and 1993 is in progress—then the agent can now also audit 1994. This year will appear on the computer screen as soon as the IRS gets your file. Now the IRS has until April 15, 1998 to complete the audit for the 1994 tax year. The next April 15, assuming the audit is still in progress—and it often is—the IRS can start auditing the 1995 return, and so on ad infinitum. Sadly, there is absolutely nothing you can do if the IRS wants to continue auditing you forever, year after year. The limitations are exceeded one year at a time, and if you do not give them an extension to finish their work for each year, they will simply close the year when it is due, and go on to auditing the next year. Usually the audit does not go on forever, but long audits, covering four or more tax years, are not uncommon. The Service strongly encourages this practice. Do not confuse this with the limitation on the IRS not to audit the same item on a third year if the item was audited on either of the previous two years and no additional tax was due. This is often circumvented in the open years approach, first, because the audits are done at the same time (these aren't new audits generated by the computer, but rather a continuation to other years of one audit), and second because it is easy for the IRS to find additional tax for at least *some* item in a given year, and then go on to other years.

Admittedly, not filing a return while an audit is in progress may not always help you, especially if the IRS is really out to get you, since eventually the extensions you request will expire and you will have to file. If an audit truly drags on, this may happen. However, remember that you are dealing with an extremely inefficient bureaucracy. Usually, buying more time will greatly improve your position, and in most cases an extension will carry you to the end of the audit and you will not have created yet another open year for the audit cancer.

CHAPTER 12

THE COHAN RULE, AND: WHAT'S REASONABLE?

When the IRS agent is auditing your expenses to verify the validity of the deductions you claimed on your return, he or she will be looking for receipts to substantiate every item. For every expense you incurred, you are expected to provide an actual receipt. You are also expected to substantiate your reason for claiming the expense. Was the expense you incurred necessary for conducting your business? When a claim cannot be substantiated by showing a receipt, or when the reason for the expense is not accepted, the agent will *disallow* the claimed expense—the assumption being that you did not incur the expense, or that it wasn't necessary for your business or employment. When everything is totalled, you may realize that you have lost a significant amount of claimed deductions against your tax bill. Then the interest is added, and penalties—you are being punished for having made false claims to the IRS.

But no one should be expected to have perfect records! We are human beings, not machines that collect receipts every moment of our lives. Some records may get lost or misplaced and you shouldn't lose every deduction you

IN LOOKING
AT YOUR
DEDUCTIONS
THE IRS AGENT
HAS ONE
OBJECTIVE: TO
DISALLOW

65

can't prove with a piece of paper. The IRS does not like this line of reasoning. To it a claim without an actual receipt is a false claim. However, in 1930 the entertainer George M. Cohan (*"I'm a Yankee Doodle Dandy"*) went to court against the IRS. Cohan did not have receipts for all of his business expenses. The court took the position that even if records are not complete, the IRS should allow such expenses if they are reasonable. The court's ruling that lack of evidence does not automatically take away your right to deductions became a landmark decision. So if you can justify your expenses and they will seem reasonable given your occupation, the IRS may accept some of these deductions if pushed to do so. If you have to go to court, the court may allow an estimated value for some deductions without receipts, although these amounts will be less than the full amount you failed to prove with receipts. The Cohan rule, however, does not apply to travel and entertainment expenses, as these were viewed as easily abused for personal rather than business purposes.

THE COHAN RULE SAYS YOU MAY BE ABLE TO CLAIM SOME DEDUCTIONS WITHOUT ACTUAL RECEIPTS IF THEY SEEM REASONABLE (BUT IT'S HIGHLY ADVISABLE TO HAVE RECEIPTS FOR EVERYTHING)

It is still always the best policy to keep perfect receipts if at all possible. It is also a very good idea to keep a journal of all your expenses as back-up and reinforcement for the receipts you have. Then, if the IRS disputes some of your items, you may mention to the agent the Cohan rule, and there may be a sudden change in attitude as the agent realizes that you know the law and are willing to fight.

Beyond keeping receipts and journals to substantiate your deductions, remember that you will also have to prove to the IRS that your deductions are indeed justified for conducting your business. This accountant's mindset, even more than receipts and other substantiation, is a key to winning your audit. Your enemy is much more crafty and cynical when it comes to trying to take away your right to make your deductions than they are in questioning your receipts. In trying to do this, the IRS has a formidable legal tool in its arsenal:

THE IRS CAN DECIDE THAT YOUR BUSINESS IS A HOBBY AND FLATLY DISALLOW ALL YOUR BUSINESS DEDUCTIONS

The IRS follows some definite guidelines that it has set up in determining what is reasonable in any given category. If your deductions in a given area exceed these guidelines, then the IRS will decide that your entire category of deductions should be disallowed. If you are a farmer, and you incur high expenses in running your farm, the IRS may decide that you are a Gentleman (Gentlewoman) Farmer and will disallow all your deductions for farm expenses. This is an incredibly powerful tool of which you need to be aware. Make sure you can prove that your business is not a hobby. The IRS has a "3-out-of-5" rule for throwing out your business deductions: If in at least three out of five years your business has not shown a profit, it can be determined a hobby. While this rule is not cast in stone, the IRS puts the burden of proof for the legitimacy of a business squarely on the taxpayer. The key here is to demonstrate to the IRS that you are *trying* to make a profit—and not just using the business as a tax writeoff. Thus, in an audit of such items, the agent will want to look at other years as well—this gives the IRS an excuse to examine other open years, which sets new traps for you. The same consideration will be used in capitalization issues, for example, writing off the cost of a computer you bought one year over its expected life of several years. You should be aware of all these issues when preparing your taxes, realizing that these issues may come back to haunt you in an audit.

CHAPTER 13

EVER APPEAL

O nce the audit process is over, the IRS agent issues a report with any adjustments to your tax bill based on the audit. If you disagree with the agent's findings, you have several options. It is highly recommended that you pursue at least some of these options. It is very rarely in your best interest to agree with the IRS.

After looking at the examination report, call the agent and explain why you disagree with the findings. There is a chance that the agent will compromise with you and reduce the amount of added tax demanded. If this does not happen, ask to meet with the agent's supervisor. An IRS group manager will usually support the findings of the auditor—but not always. You now have a new chance to explain your case to the manager and, using the techniques described earlier, this time you may be successful.

The group manager has an incentive to come to your side. The reason is, as usual, statistics. The auditor's performance is judged by the IRS based on the number of cases that are closed by the taxpayer's agreement. When the taxpayer does not agree with the agent's report and goes on

IT IS ALWAYS A
GOOD IDEA
TO TRY TO MEET
THE AGENT'S
SUPERVISOR

to appeal, this costs the government money and time and makes the Service's work less efficient. Therefore, not only the agent, but also the supervisor, will look better if he or she can settle your case without an appeal. If you calmly explain your reasons, there is a chance they will come toward you. If not, you still haven't lost anything. Now would be the time for a real, official appeal to the IRS. The IRS has an administrative procedure for appealing examination results. The appeal process is simple and does not cost you anything, and in most probability your tax bill will be reduced. It is true that the appeals officer can legally review your entire file and that this process may actually increase the amount you owe. Practically speaking, however, an expanded examination is rare, so usually the appeal will reduce your bill. There is another important reason for appealing: time. The appeal process extends the time involved, and remember that time always works in your favor—anything can still go wrong and you may have to pay nothing. According to IRS statistics, appeals result in an average *reduction* of your tax bill by over 40 percent!

Clearly, the IRS does not want you to appeal. The Service has forms for any possible purpose, except for appeals! So you need to write your own protest letter to the IRS District Director in order to request an appeal of your audit results. You should do so immediately after receiving the letter notifying you of the examination report and the proposed adjustments to your tax bill. This is the "30 Day Letter," and you should act within this time limit so as not to lose the opportunity to appeal. In your letter, explain why you disagree with the audit results and include copies of the 30-day letter and the examination report. In the appeal you do not have to show that the examination results are completely false, but rather that you have an arguable position in disputing the auditor's findings. You will have several months to prepare your appeal, and you should use your time wisely. Go over everything you presented at the audit, and look for additional information. This new information, if you can find it, may make a big difference in the outcome of the appeal. Try to find new and better ways to present your case—try to provide better documentation for your deductions and claims. Think of better explanations that you can make in trying to convince the appeals officer that you are right. It may be a good idea to bring witnesses to corroborate your claims.

The appeals officer who will hear your case is probably older and more experienced than the auditor, and has more latitude in deciding your case. The appeals officer is judged by how many cases he or she *settles* with the taxpayer, rather than on backing up the original auditor's report. If you want to make a deal with the IRS, now may be the time to do so to your advantage, especially if you have some new documentation. The appeals officer makes a serious assessment of the hazard of litigation. The officer will weigh your perceived determination to go to court should the appeal not go as you hoped it would, and will also make an assessment of whether or not the government will lose the case should it go to court.

In recent years, most of the resources of the IRS have been allocated to computerization and other modernization efforts rather than for filling the ranks of IRS attorneys ready to do battle in tax court. Since legal resources are

IT USUALLY PAYS (OFTEN QUITE HANDSOMELY) TO APPEAL

THE IRS DOES NOT WANT YOU TO GO TO COURT—USE THIS FACT TO YOUR ADVANTAGE

71

scarce, the IRS will try—whenever possible—to avoid going to court with you. In your appeal, you must demonstrate to the appeals officer that you have a *chance* of winning the case if it goes to tax court.

Start doing some *legal* research of the issues involved, in preparation for a possible court case. Look for precedents or legal rulings in cases that are similar to yours so you can see what the courts' decisions have been on the issues at stake. The fact that you are well-prepared to go to court may convince the appeals officer to negotiate a compromise decision in your case. Over 85% of all appeals are settled without having to go to court. However, in case you fail in your appeal, you should definitely consider going to tax court.

In small cases (less than $10,000 in dispute for any one year), no attorney is necessary. The tax court in such cases works like small claims court where you present your case in an informal way, and the judge makes a decision. The tax court is independent of the IRS, and it offers you yet another chance of presenting your case and beating the results of the audit. Going to court will, again, buy you more time—filing a petition to go to court will get you a year or more before the tax bill is due. Interest will be running on the amount you owe. However, you can stop the interest clock from ticking by paying the IRS the amount they claim is due, and later getting back this amount or part of it if you win your case.

READINESS TO SUE WILL GIVE YOU YET ANOTHER CHANCE TO SETTLE YOUR CASE WITH THE IRS, WITHOUT THE TRIAL

Most often, the IRS is not certain to win its case against you, so going to court will give you yet another opportu-

Chapter 13

72

nity to settle the case without a trial. In fact, over 80% of the cases that are filed against the IRS are settled without a trial. Going to court is not likely to bring you a complete victory; however, about half the cases that do go to court bring at least some reduction of your original bill.

Filing a Tax Court Petition without valid grounds can get you in trouble, as such cases are considered frivolous. Going to court without justification can result in a fine of up to $5,000. If you do have a good case, by all means file a petition. After you file, you will hear from the IRS attorney handling the case, and this will give you yet another chance to settle your case with the IRS without an actual trial. As long as the judge has not made a ruling, you can always settle the case with the IRS attorney.

If you do go to trial, prepare your case well before your day in court. Bring documents and witnesses if you can. Make your presentation short and to the point. Consider giving the judge a written outline of your arguments as to why you believe you do not owe the tax. The judge's decision will be made known to you in about a month or so, and that decision is final, without possibility of further appeal. The ruling is usually brief, listing the amount of tax and any penalties that may apply.

What we described above applies to the Tax Court Small Claims procedure. If your case is not small, you will need an attorney. There are also other courts where your case against the IRS may be heard. You can pay the amount the IRS says you owe and then *sue for a refund* in a Federal District Court or in the Claims Court in Washington, D.C. In both places you will need an attorney.

CHAPTER 14

THE TAX COLLECTOR

T he collection division of the IRS is a hungry beast, programmed like a shark: eat as quickly and as much as possible. Whenever the IRS determines that you owe more money, you will get a first request to pay the determined amount. If payment is not received in 30 to 60 days, the IRS issues a series of reminders over several weeks. If all of these are ignored, the IRS then sends you a final notice, after which it can start enforced collection of the tax. Levy (seizure) orders can now be issued to third parties that have money belonging to you—employers and banks where you have accounts. If you cannot pay, you should respond in writing to the requests. If you specifically ask for 60 days to make payment (the maximum allowed), and include a small payment with your request to show your intention to pay, you will buy more time. Often this may delay the hungry shark from coming after you by as much as several months or more.

THE TAX COLLECTOR HAS AN IMPRESSIVE ARRAY OF WEAPONS AT HIS OR HER DISPOSAL

If you fail to pay the Service Center, which issues the notices, your file will be transferred to the IRS's Automated Collection System (ACS). This is a *computer system* designed to collect the tax. The ACS is a sinister resident of cyberspace. It is a sophisticated computing network designed to collect information about you from as many sources as possible: state and local agencies such as motor vehicle departments, licensing offices, etc., as well as banks and registries of all kinds. The ACS is the machinery that locates any asset you own or money you have that can then be fed to the shark. As soon as the ACS locates a levy source, it sends a notice to seize. It is impossible for a taxpayer to deal with this vicious, impersonal computer system. The best you can do is to try to have the IRS District Office get back your file from the ACS so you can negotiate a payment plan with them, and buy more time and have the seizure stopped. It is very difficult to stop a levy against your bank accounts.

Once property you own has been seized, you may still redeem it from the IRS if you can make payment of the tax demanded and the expenses incurred in seizing the property. You may also convince the IRS to release the levy if you can show your intent to pay.

DO EVERYTHING TO AVOID HAVING YOUR FILE SENT TO THE ACS

JEOPARDY ASSESSMENT

A jeopardy assessment is probably the most powerful collection tool of the IRS, and the one most open to abuse of the taxpayer—its use amounts to sheer terrorism.

When the IRS makes a jeopardy assessment against you, the rules of the game are gone. The IRS does not owe you even the courtesy of a notice. The jeopardy assessment allows the IRS to immediately demand full payment of the amount it claims is due, or the posting of a bond for this

A JEOPARDY ASSESSMENT CAN BE MADE WITHOUT PRIOR NOTICE TO THE TAXPAYER

75

full amount. The amount of a jeopardy assessment is almost always larger than the actual tax liability. If the taxpayer does not pay, the IRS can *immediately* begin seizing any property, assets, money belonging to the taxpayer, *before* the taxpayer even has the chance to object, ask for an explanation, or make any form of appeal. It is, of course, one of the greatest disgraces of our society that a practice such as the jeopardy assessment is allowed. One expects such things in countries where human rights are violated, but make no mistake about it—the government of the United States of America can take away your property without notice, without explanation, and without leaving you any recourse.

The IRS may invoke a jeopardy assessment against you any time it believes that tax collection will be *jeopardized* by delay. If you are audited by the IRS and the agent conducting the investigation becomes suspicious that in case additional tax is assessed against you, you will flee the country, a jeopardy assessment may be made. Auditors will sometimes abuse their power and threaten a taxpayer that if he or she does not cooperate a jeopardy assessment will be made. Sometimes the agent will be bluffing, other times he or she may actually mean it. The potential abuse of power is virtually unlimited.

Legally, the IRS can invoke a jeopardy assessment if it *suspects* one of the following:

    1. The taxpayer is preparing to leave the country, or

    2. The taxpayer plans to transfer his or her assets

to a destination outside the country where the IRS may not be able to seize them, or

3. The taxpayer is preparing to hide assets, spend his or her money, or transfer monies and property to others, or

4. The taxpayer may become financially insolvent.

An IRS examiner does not have the authority to order a jeopardy assessment, but a regional or a district director of the IRS has this power. The agent must send a recommendation for the jeopardy assessment to the higher-ups in the IRS bureaucracy, who can then make the assessment. A jeopardy assessment short-circuits any judicial review of the position of the IRS in the audit by allowing the assessment to be made *without* first sending the taxpayer a notice of deficiency.

A JEOPARDY ASSESSMENT WILL DEPRIVE YOU OF ANY RIGHT TO DEFEND YOUR PROPERTY

At times, IRS agents will threaten a taxpayer with a jeopardy assessment if the taxpayer should refuse to sign the form allowing the IRS to extend its investigation beyond the usual three-year limit. The IRS says that if you don't sign away your rights they will take away even more of your rights—in fact, strip you of virtually all your rights to due process. While it is questionable whether the IRS can legally do this, there have been some old cases where a jeopardy assessment was made in such circumstances. Schnepper (1978, p. 2) recounts a number of horror stories where the IRS' power to issue a jeopardy assessment was abused. One of them is about a Major in the United States Army whose wife needed a life-saving operation. Four months before any tax was due, the Major wrote to the IRS, explaining that he worried about not having enough money to pay his taxes because of his wife's operation, and requesting a meeting with an IRS agent to arrange a way for him to pay off his taxes for the year. The IRS swiftly responded to the letter with a "jeopardy and termination assessment," freezing the Major's bank account just when he needed the money for his wife's operation. Burnham (1989, p. 64) tells the bizzare story of Sharon Willits, an attractive Florida divorcee who was investigated by the IRS in 1973. When it was determined that Ms. Willits had not filed a tax return in four years, the IRS arbitrarily decided that her annual income was $60,000, and issued a jeopardy assessment against her assets in the amount of $25,000. On appeal, it was determined that Ms. Willits was actually living on monthly alimony payments of $135 and the $2,000 proceeds from the sale of the house she had won as part of her divorce settlement. The Court of Appeals further concluded that the IRS' seisure of Ms. Willits' property was based on a purely fictitious income assessment.

CHAPTER 15

AVOIDING AN AUDIT: AN OVERVIEW

Now that you've seen how bad things can get for you once you are audited, and have considered ways of fighting back, it's time to begin our discussion of how to avoid the ordeal altogether—how to minimize your taxes while also minimizing the chance of an audit: in short, how to beat the IRS at its own game!

Remember that the information on your tax return is entered into the IRS computer by keypunch operators who are hired part-time, poorly trained, and pushed by their supervisors to enter the data quickly. Your return is therefore keypunched in an extremely short time. It stands to reason that the number of numerical elements from each return entered into the computer to be analyzed by the DIF—the Discriminant Function procedure used by the IRS to determine who should be audited—is not very large (although the IRS would have you think the DIF is very complicated...). My own analysis of a sample of 1,289 audited and unaudited returns in chase of the DIF indeed confirms this belief. In fact, my extensive computer analyses on a Cray-2 supercomputer revealed that a handful of *variables* account for about 90% of all audits. We will con-

A RELATIVELY
SMALL NUMBER
OF VARIABLES IN
THE RETURN
TRIGGER 90% OF
ALL AUDITS

centrate on understanding these variables in the following chapters, and on showing how these variables should be measured and manipulated to reduce the chance of an audit to a minimum.

What about the remaining 10%? These audits are caused by factors extraneous to the actual DIF analysis done by the IRS. Mathematical errors caught by the computer will trigger a mail audit that may expand to a full-scale audit (but may also prevent one). Previous audits raise the DIF and can cause new audits. Then there is the relatively small probability that the return will be chosen purely at random for a TCMP audit. Certain professions are likely to be audited because from time to time the IRS makes policy decisions to look more carefully at one industry or another. Also, any *inconsistencies* on your tax return will raise the chance of an audit. These include disagreement of what you report on your federal tax return with what you report on your state tax return; wrong names or other information about your dependents; large changes in information from year to year, and other factors. All of these comprise a fraction of all audits. While arithmetical errors can be avoided, and so can the "nice-numbers" trap, one can hardly help belonging to a particular profession or having been audited in the past. We will therefore concentrate on avoiding the factors that cause the majority, 90%, of audits.

THINGS TO AVOID AND TO CHECK YOUR RETURN CAREFULLY FOR:

1. Nice, whole numbers (such as: $2,000, instead

of $1,988.91)

2. Inconsistencies across years (If your daughter changed her name in 1995, let the IRS know about it so they don't audit you, suspecting a fake dependent when comparing your 1994 return with the 1995 return.)

3. Agreement of state return information with that of the federal one.

4. Inexplicable large shifts in income and/or expenses from year to year.

The approach we will take is that of *quality control*. We will carefully construct our tax return, first checking for the minor problems listed above. Then we will look at the variables that cause the majority of audits and find ways to minimize their impact. The variables are important *ratios*. These ratios were detected by the computer when I instructed it to try every imaginable combination of variables to find the mix of factors that is best in explaining the difference between returns that are audited and those that are not. This is where an artificial intelligence approach, and a supercomputer, were needed. With 1,289 returns, 631 of which were audited and 658 unaudited, and with a large number of possible combinations to check, it was imperative to find an efficient estimation method. Artificial intelligence is the art of making the computer emulate human thought. To achieve this aim, I used a program that made the computer "think." The computer tried a sequence of variables and looked for the best separation between the two groups of returns. When the best single variable was found, combinations of this variable with all other variables were tested. Then the best combination was checked against combinations with the remaining variables, and so on. At any point in the process, the computer would check the validity of variables chosen earlier in the presence of ones chosen later. If a variable or combination of variables were no longer the best, they were dropped. The result of this exhaustive search was the ratios to be discussed later.

We will also give some important rules that seem to work very well in general in helping to reduce the chance of an audit—regardless of the factor causing the audit! These are given in the next two chapters.

CHAPTER 16

EVER DELAY!

The IRS allows taxpayers to file their income tax returns *late*. The first such extension is, in fact, *automatic!* That is, all the taxpayer has to do is to file the appropriate form (Form 4868) by April 15, and he or she is *guaranteed* an extension of the time to file. This first extension pushes the deadline to file the return from April 15 four months ahead to August 15. Of course, taxes are due on April 15 and must be paid then. You should therefore estimate the tax you owe for the year and send the IRS a check for that amount accompanying the extension request form. Interest will be charged on all late payments. There is also a penalty in case of underpayment of over 10% of the taxbill settled with the extended return.

There is also a *second* extension of time that is possible, but must be approved by the IRS. This is done by filing Form 2688 with an *explanation* of the reasons why you need the extension. There must be valid reasons that will be acceptable to the Service before it will approve the request. This second extension will further push the time to file two months, to October 15.

THE IRS ALLOWS AN AUTOMATIC, NO-QUESTIONS-ASKED EXTENSION TO FILE BY AUGUST 15

A SECOND
EXTENSION OF
THE TIME TO
FILE, WITH
REASONS,
MAY BE
GRANTED,
PUSHING THE
DEADLINE TO
OCTOBER 15

Again, remember that the estimated tax, as close to the actual liability as possible, must be paid on April 15.

The data in my study strongly indicate that filing late reduces the chance of an audit, as I will show below. This statistical finding makes a lot of sense. Remember that the IRS game is a *timed* game, and that time—by the very nature of the audit process—works in your favor.

Let's look again at the time frame for audits. Most individual taxpayers file their returns by April 15. Five percent of the taxpayers file for the automatic extension, and one percent file for a second extension to October 15. With 95% of the returns keypunched and entered into the system by mid- to late April, the IRS machine—ever pressed for time—is ready to roll. The DIF starts working on the computer records of over 100 million taxpayers right away. Now, the resources of the agency and other factors dictate that roughly one percent of all tax returns be audited. This percentage varies from state to state and across national regions. In some places it is 1.5%, in others as low as 0.5%. Once the returns that have been identified by the DIF as audit-requiring are tagged, there is no time to waste, because of the three-year limit on completing the audits. It therefore stands to reason that late-filed returns may be scrutinized by the DIF *after* the allotted quota of roughly one percent nationally has been reached and no audits are to follow. It is even possible that late-filed returns may not be analyzed by the DIF at all. Even if you will be audited when you filed your return late, time is now more likely to run out on the IRS, and this could benefit you. Your audit may even be dropped if some unusual further delays and other circumstances should intervene.

Unless there are other considerations, such as wanting to get your refund as quickly as possible, you should definitely file for an extension. In addition to the automatic extension, look for any legitimate excuse you can find (although it *must* be convincing or the IRS will reject it) and request a *second extension* to October 15. In my study, returns that otherwise (for the reasons explained in following chapters) *should* have been audited by the IRS were not. This was especially true for returns that were filed after a *second* extension to October 15. Out of 1,289 returns, 73 were filed late, and of these, not one was audited. This fact, alone, may not mean much since the overall audit probability is only about one percent. However, twelve of the 73 late-filed returns reported information that—based on the rules explained in the following chapters—would have made them likely to be audited. Seventeen returns had ratio-based audit probability of over 80 percent. The fact that these returns were *not* audited certainly suggests that filing late reduces the audit vulnerability. Twelve of the late-filed returns were filed on October 15 (using a second extension) and none were audited. Of these twelve returns, three had ratio-based audit probabilities of 98 percent, 99.7 percent, and 99.9 percent, respectively. The last return, in fact, violated very strongly *two* of the ratio-rules I give in the following chapters. I believe that these facts speak for themselves.

Remember that the rules given here and elsewhere in this book are *statistical* ones. They work in general by reducing the *probability* of an audit. They do not give you a

FILE THE AUTOMATIC EXTENSION REQUEST AND LOOK FOR ANY LEGITIMATE REASON FOR ASKING FOR A SECOND EXTENSION, TO FILE BY OCTOBER 15 *guarantee* that you will not be audited. Since statistics is the name of the game, *no one* can give you a guarantee— the best we can do is to minimize the chance that your return will be audited.

CHAPTER 17

ALWAYS EXPLAIN, OVER AND OVER

The second general rule that emerged from my analysis of a large number of returns—and even more important than the rule in the previous chapter—is that *explanations* go a very long way in reducing your audit probability.

Remember that computers, however useful, do not conduct audits. *People* are the ones who ultimately decide whether or not to audit you, and it is *people* who actually conduct the audit. Once the DIF calls up your return and decides that you should be audited, your file is picked up by a classifier, an employee of the IRS trained at determining whether or not to take the computer's recommendation to audit you. The IRS policy decision, at present, is to audit only about 10% of the returns tagged by the DIF.

This means that *even if your return looks bad from a statistical point of view*, and the computer has indeed identified your return as one warranting an audit, your chances of an actual audit are only 10%! What determines your fate now? The answer lies in how your return looks to the human eye, not the machine.

ONLY 10% OF THE RETURNS TAGGED BY THE COMPUTER ARE ACTUALLY AUDITED

87

MAKE SURE
YOUR RETURN
LOOKS AS
GOOD AS
POSSIBLE TO THE
HUMAN EYE

This means that you should include as many convincing, valid written *explanations* for everything you claim on your return. If one of the ratios described in the following chapters goes critical on you and triggers the IRS computer to spit out your return, you want the person looking at your file to say: "AHA! Now I understand why there are all these deductions on Schedule C. This all looks fine to me. Do not audit".

This point cannot be over-emphasized in this book. You want the IRS people looking at your return to be convinced that you have prepared it correctly, however unusual your circumstances may be from a statistical point of view. If you pass the test of scrutiny by an IRS employee, there will never be an audit.

YOU WANT THE
IRS EMPLOYEE
LOOKING AT
YOUR RETURN
TO UNDERSTAND
WHY YOU HAVE
PREPARED IT AS
YOU DID, AND
THEREFORE TO
DECIDE THAT
NO AUDIT IS
NECESSARY

To achieve this goal, you must think about everything *while preparing* your tax return. Make notes on reasons for every expense you incurred, explain every deduction, loss, or contribution. Then type your reasons and explanations neatly on sheets that look professional. It is advisable to use a computer. This will convince the IRS employee that you have indeed done a thorough job of both calculating your deductions and validating them. Include your explanation sheets as supplements. An example is shown here.

SUPPLEMENT No. 1
JOB-RELATED EXPENSES OTHER THAN TRAVEL, MEALS AND ENTERTAINMENT

A. Educational Expenses:

These expenses were incurred as part of my attendance at a seminar on improved direct-marketing methods at the University of California on May 3-18 to learn new techniques necessary for my job as Marketing Director at my company. The seminar was not necessary for meeting minimum requirements for holding my job, nor was it necessary for qualifying for a new job. The seminar improved my job performance.

Tuition at Seminar	$1,560.00
Books	$ 275.00
Supplies	$ 105.00
Total:	$1,940.00

B. Equipment:

1. Home Computer and peripherals.

The computer is used 95% for my work: preparing reports, doing budgets, forecasting sales. Purchased 3/17/94.

Purchase price: $6,125.00
Expensing Deduction: 95% x 6,125 = $5,818.75

2. Other equipment purchased in 1994:

calculator	$ 89.50
computer software	$ 97.25
Total:	$186.75

89

3. Books. These are needed to further my mastery of marketing methods required for my company to stay competitive in its field.

Twenty eight books were purchased in 1994, names and prices follow.

Total cost: $672.13

NEAT-LOOKING, COMPUTER-PREPARED RETURNS WITH LOTS OF COMMENTS AND EXPLANA-TIONS ON ATTACHED SHEETS GO A LONG WAY IN CONVINCING THE IRS THAT YOU NEED NOT BE AUDITED

Returns that look neat, are typed or prepared on a computer and that have ample explanations throughout on additional pages will reduce your audit probability. Twenty-two returns in my sample had a ratio-based audit probability of over 75% but were not audited because they included neatly-typed, clear explanations as supplements. Four returns in the sample, which had a ratio-based audit probability of less than half a percent were audited, and all of them were sloppily handwritten (possibly, the information on at least some of these returns was incorrectly input into the computer, leading to the audit).

CHAPTER 18

DEVELOPING YOUR PERSONAL ACCOUNTING RATIOS

W e now get to the actual *variables* in the return that trigger the DIF and make the computer decide that you should be audited. All the variables that were picked by my sophisticated statistical and artificial-intelligence algorithms used in analyzing the sample of 1,289 returns (in a way that mimics the DIF used by the IRS) are *ratios* of amounts that appear in various locations on the tax return. I will now explain how you should compute these ratios while preparing your return, and test them following the rules I give in the following chapter.

THE MAIN VARIABLES THAT TRIGGER THE DIF ARE RATIOS

We will define a *personal accounting ratio* (PAR), as the ratio of two quantities that appear on your return. The ratios are numbers that will be decimals between 0 and 1 if the quantity in the numerator is smaller than the quantity in the denominator. If the numerator is greater than the denominator, the ratio will be a number (with decimals) that is greater than 1.00.

PAR for SCHEDULE A:

Let us look at the first PAR, the PAR for Schedule A. Look

at the bottom of the page on Schedule A. The last line is: "Total Itemized Deductions." Suppose that when you finished preparing your Schedule A, that figure comes out to be $15,000. (Beware! This is used only for demonstration purposes; in reality avoid "nice" numbers.) Now look at the figure you report on line 31 of your 1040 tax form. This is your Adjusted Gross Income. Suppose that this figure is $60,000. We define the Schedule A PAR as:

$$PAR(A) \; = \; \frac{\text{Total Itemized Deductions on Schedule A}}{\text{Adjusted Gross Income on Form 1040}}$$

$$= \$15,000/\$60,000 \; = \; 0.25.$$

Why ratios? When a large number of possible variables were entered into a computer in order to analyze the returns in a way that discriminates between audited and unaudited returns, I discovered that *ratios* were statistically most significant. This makes a lot of sense because *ratios* are also *percents*. To answer the question: "What is reasonable?" it is best to look at ratios. If your income is $60,000 and you have Schedule A deductions of $15,000, then your deductions amount to 25% (the ratio is 0.25) of your income. If, on the other hand, your income was only $20,000 and your Schedule A deductions were, as before, $15,000, then your PAR is 15,000/20,000=0.75, or 75% of your income! The little that is publicly written about the IRS's secret DIF says that it considers different criteria for different income levels. This confirms that ratios are indeed the way to go, as they allow a comparison that accounts for different incomes.

PAR for SCHEDULE C:

We define your personal accounting ratio for Schedule C as:

$$PAR(C) = \frac{\text{Total Expenses on Schedule C (Line 28 + Line 30)}}{\text{Gross Income on Schedule C (Line 7)}}$$

If you file no Schedule C, your PAR(C)=0.

Suppose that you had total expenses on Line 28 of Schedule C amounting to $25,000, and that you had additional expenses for business use of your home (Line 30 of Schedule C) amounting to $8,000. Now let's assume that your gross income on Schedule C (Line 7) was $100,000. Then your personal accounting ratio for Schedule C is:

$$PAR(C) = (25,000 + 8,000)/100,000$$
$$= 0.33 \text{ (or 33%)}$$

What about losses? How are these accounted for by the PAR? The answer is that here is where the PAR exceeds 1.00. Let's look at an example. Suppose your business reported on Schedule C had gross income of $30,000 but your expenses reported on Line 28 were $50,000, and you did not use your home (Line 30 expenses are zero). Your personal accounting ratio for Schedule C is:

$$PAR(C) = 50,000/30,000$$

93

$$= \quad 1.667 \text{ (or } 166.7\%)$$

It is interesting to note that the IRS's DIF will pick you up for an audit long before you show a loss. as in this example. The trigger points are well below the break-even PAR of 1.00.

PAR for SCHEDULE F:

Your personal accounting ratio for Schedule F (assuming you file a Schedule F, otherwise it is defined as zero) is as follows:

$$PAR(F) = \frac{\text{Total Expenses on Schedule F (Line 35)}}{\text{Gross Income on Schedule F (Line 11)}}$$

If you have a farm and you incurred total expenses of $78,000 running your farm for the year and your gross income from the farm was $200,000, then your personal accounting ratio for Schedule F is computed as:

$$PAR(F) = \quad 78,000/200,000$$
$$= \quad 0.39 \text{ (or } 39\%)$$

Suppose that your farm lost a lot of money this year. Your expenses amounted to $120,000 while your gross income from the farm was only $20,000. In this case your personal accounting ratio for Schedule F is:

$$PAR(F) \quad = \quad 120,000/20,000$$
$$= \quad 6.00 \text{ (or } 600\%)$$

Chapter 18   Again, a loss will make your PAR greater than 1.00.

USING YOUR PARs TO DEFEAT THE DIF

In the following chapter we present statistically-derived points that trigger the IRS's DIF to tag your return for an audit. These are noted on the DIF-Buster Gauges for the different income tax Schedules. Use them as you would use the speedometer in your car. For each PAR there will be a "Caution Point" and a "Critical Point." We refer to the area after you exceed the Caution Point but before your ratio reaches the Critical Point as the "Caution Zone." The area of increasingly higher ratios beyond the Critical Point is referred to as the "Critical Zone." Once you pass the Caution Point and enter the Caution Zone, your probability of an audit increases as your ratio becomes greater. At the Critical Point, the IRS computer is *known* (from analysis of the data) to actually pick out your return to be audited. (Then, of course, the classifier will look at the return, so an audit is not a certainty even yet.)

CHAPTER 19

DIF-BUSTER GAUGES FOR SCHEDULES A, C, AND F

MOST AUDITS
ARE CAUSED BY
A RETURN
REACHING OR
EXCEEDING
THE CRITICAL
POINT FOR A PAR
OF AT LEAST
ONE OF
THE THREE
SCHEDULES: A,
C, AND F

T his is probably the most important chapter in this book. Over 90 percent of the audits in my sample (569 audited returns, out of a total of 631 audited returns) were determined to have been caused by the returns' exceeding the Critical Points for the PAR of either Schedule A, Schedule C, Schedule F (less frequently than A and C), or combinations of any two of these schedules or all three of them.

Published reports by the IRS inadvertently agree with these findings, at least indirectly. While the reported audit rate for all returns is roughly one percent, the audit rate for returns with a Schedule C is four times as high, a close second are returns with a Schedule A, and at a somewhat lower rate but still more than double the overall average of one percent audit rate are returns with a Schedule F.

DIF-BUSTER GAUGE FOR SCHEDULE A:

Chapter 19

Compute your personal accounting ratio for Schedule A as explained in the previous chapter. Now carry out the simple test below:

> IS PAR(A) GREATER THAN OR EQUAL TO 0.44
> (or 44%)? IF YES, YOU HAVE JUST EXCEEDED
> THE CRITICAL POINT FOR SCHEDULE A. THE
> DIF-FORMULA INSIDE THE IRS COMPUTER
> WILL CERTAINLY KICK OUT YOUR RETURN
> FOR POSSIBLE AUDIT

The Caution Zone:

> THE CAUTION ZONE FOR AN AUDIT BASED ON
> PAR(A) IS APPROACHED AS YOUR RETURN GETS
> CLOSE TO HAVING PAR(A) EQUAL TO 0.35 (or
> 35%)

Returns with PAR(A) less than 0.35 are not very likely to be audited; returns with PAR(A) between 0.35 and 0.44 have a relatively high audit probability (at least as far as computer-tagging); and returns with PAR(A) of above 0.44 are certain to be computer-tagged for audit. Figure 2 shows our DIF-Buster gauge for Schedule A.

Figure 2
DIF-BUSTER GAUGE FOR SCHEDULE A

DIF-BUSTER GAUGE FOR SCHEDULE C:

Compute your personal accounting ratio for Schedule C as explained in the previous chapter. Now carry out the simple test below:

> IS PAR(C) GREATER THAN OR EQUAL
> TO 0.67 (or 67%)?
> IF YES, YOU HAVE JUST EXCEEDED THE
> CRITICAL POINT FOR SCHEDULE C.
> THE DIF-FORMULA INSIDE THE IRS COMPUTER
> WILL CERTAINLY KICK OUT YOUR RETURN FOR
> POSSIBLE AUDIT

The Caution Zone:

> THE CAUTION ZONE FOR AN AUDIT BASED ON
> PAR(C) IS APPROACHED AS YOUR RETURN GETS
> CLOSE TO HAVING PAR(C) EQUAL TO 0.52 (or
> 52%)

Returns with PAR(C) less than 0.52 are not very likely to be audited; returns with PAR(C) between 0.52 and 0.67 have a relatively high audit probability (at least as far as computer-tagging); and returns with PAR(C) of above 0.67 are certain to be computer-tagged for audit. Our Schedule C DIF-Buster gauge is shown in Figure 3.

Figure 3

DIF-BUSTER GAUGE FOR SCHEDULE C

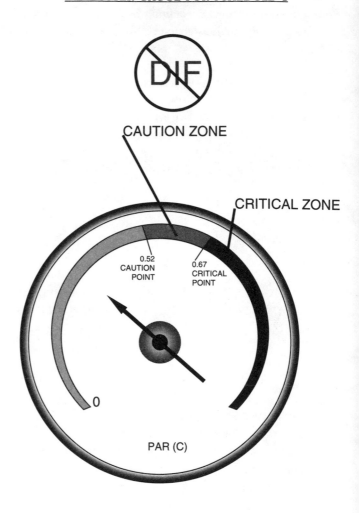

PAR (C)

DIF-BUSTER GAUGE FOR SCHEDULE F:

Compute your personal accounting ratio for Schedule F as explained in the previous chapter. Now carry out the simple test below:

> IS PAR(F) GREATER THAN OR EQUAL TO 0.71 (or 71%)?
> IF YES, YOU HAVE JUST EXCEEDED THE CRITICAL POINT FOR SCHEDULE F. THE DIF-FORMULA INSIDE THE IRS COMPUTER WILL CERTAINLY KICK OUT YOUR RETURN FOR POSSIBLE AUDIT

The Caution Zone:

> THE CAUTION ZONE FOR AN AUDIT BASED ON PAR(F) IS APPROACHED AS YOUR RETURN GETS CLOSE TO HAVING PAR(F) EQUAL TO 0.59 (or 59%)

Returns with PAR(F) less than 0.59 are not very likely to be audited; returns with PAR(F) between 0.59 and 0.71 have a relatively high audit probability (at least as far as computer-tagging); and returns with PAR(F) of above 0.71 are certain to be computer-tagged for audit. Our DIF-Buster gauge for Schedule F is shown in Figure 4.

Figure 4
DIF-BUSTER GAUGE FOR SCHEDULE F

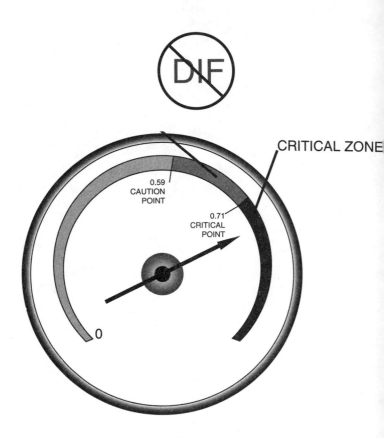

COMBINATIONS OF SCHEDULE A AND SCHEDULE C:

If your return contains both a Schedule A and a Schedule C, a test is also recommended for the combination of the two schedules. The Caution Point is 1.05 and it applies to the combination: PAR(C) + 1.5 PAR(A). That is, we want to test the inequality:

$$PAR(C) + 1.5[PAR(A)] < 1.05 \text{ (or } 105\%,$$
if percentages are used for the two PARs)

If the inequality above is *not* satisfied, that is, if the combination obtained by adding your PAR(C) to one-and-a-half of PAR(A) *exceeds* the point 1.05, the IRS computer may tag your return for an audit (1.05 is the Caution Point for the combination). To be safe, you must check both the combination above *and* do the separate tests for Schedules A and C given earlier.

Note that the separate tests above are more important than the combined test.

WHEN BOTH SCHEDULE A AND C ARE PRESENT, TEST EACH OF THEM SEPARATELY USING THE DIF-BUSTING-GAUGES ABOVE, AND DO THE COMBINATION TEST.

CHAPTER 20

USING THE DIF-BUSTER GAUGES, AND OTHER HINTS

T he DIF-buster prescriptions in the previous chapter should be very useful for you in trying to audit-proof your tax return. Here is where the ideas of quality-control come in. When you prepare your tax return, compute the various PARs that are appropriate. Then check your PARs against the Caution Zone levels and the Critical Points. Suppose that your Schedule A PAR falls within the Caution Zone. This means that you have an increased chance of an audit based on the ratio of your total deductions on Schedule A as compared with your adjusted gross income. Now look carefully at all the items in your Schedule A. One of these items, or more than one, is the cause for this inflation of the PAR(A).

Once you have identified the cause, you have several alternatives. First, it may be that your entry on the schedule was simply in error, in which case correcting the error solves the problem. Assuming there is no error, you may want to include detailed explanations of the particular deductions that inflate the PAR. This way, when the IRS classifier looks at your return he or she will hopefully decide that the explanation and documentation you provided are satisfactory and you will not be audited. There is also another option, which may be viable in some situations. If you have both a Schedule A and a Schedule C, perhaps you have included some expenses on your Schedule A that could have been listed legitimately on the Schedule C instead. For example, you listed office supplies used both as an employee of a company and for your side business on your Schedule A, and they could fit just as well on your Schedule C. If your PAR(A) will be reduced without affecting adversely your PAR(C), then shift the expense. Shifting items around may give you all the deductions to which you are entitled *without* breaching the limits on the PARs and thus getting you closer to an audit. Of course one policy, which may be used in conjunction with any of the others, is to file late—ask for an extension of time to file. This should also help in reducing the audit probability.

WHAT ABOUT OTHER SCHEDULES AND DEDUCTIONS?

Schedule B:
Schedule B did not come up as statistically significant in the analysis that traced the DIF used by the IRS (two audits seem to have been caused by mismatched information provided on Schedule B). This does not mean that the DIF ignores Schedule B information. Schedule B lists interest and dividend income. All such income is very easily verifiable by the IRS—it is reported to the IRS by financial institutions. The caution here is a simple one:

BE SURE THAT WHAT YOU CLAIM AS INTEREST
AND DIVIDENDS AGREES COMPLETELY WITH THE
INFORMATION THE IRS RECEIVES FROM OTHER
SOURCES

REFILING TO
REDUCE INTEREST
OR DIVIDEND
INCOME BY
$2,000 OR MORE
WILL CAUSE AN
AUDIT

The IRS has special policies for its agents on how to deal with *amended returns*, that is, returns that are refiled after the original has been filed, to report some newly discovered change in favor of the taxpayer. In dealing with amended returns, the IRS agent is instructed to audit any return with a *decrease* of $2,000 or more on Schedule B.

Schedule D:

Schedule D reports capital gains and losses. Here, too, all the information you report may be verified by the IRS based on information reported to it from other sources. This is why my sample did not contain any audits caused by Schedule D information. As with Schedule B, you should be careful that the information you provide is identical to what the IRS already knows about you.

BE SURE THAT
WHAT YOU
CLAIM AS
CAPITAL GAINS/
LOSSES AGREES
COMPLETELY
WITH THE INFOR-
MATION THE IRS
RECEIVES FROM
OTHER SOURCES

Here, too, the IRS has additional strict rules for its agents on how to deal with amended returns that report a decrease in capital gains as compared with the originally filed return. An audit is mandated when the amounts involved are at least $10,000.

AN AMENDED
RETURN WITH A
DECREASE IN
CAPITAL GAINS
OR AN INCREASE
IN LOSS OF
$10,000 OR
MORE WILL
CAUSE AN AUDIT

OTHER RED FLAGS

1. Bad Debt:

This is an item the IRS can question because it is easily abused. Reporting an unrepayable debt may increase your audit probability. Five audited returns in my sample reported bad debt. Only one unaudited return in my sample reported bad debt.

2. Casualty Loss:

This, too, is a questionable item that may cause the IRS to audit your return. This will be especially true if you forget to deduct $100.00 from the casualty amount, as required by the tax code. None in my sample fell in this category.

3. Medical Expenses Limit:

The tax code allows you to write off only medical expenses that exceed 7.5% of your adjusted gross income. Violating this rule may cause your return to be audited. The IRS is well aware of the potential for abuse of medical expense deductions. It is therefore important to be able to show that the medical expenses you claim were not paid by your insurance company. Five returns in my sample were audited because the reported medical expenses did not exceed the required minimum percentage of the adjusted gross income.

4. Charitable Contributions:

"Excessive" charitable contributions reported on your return—that is, exceeding the limits provided by law—will make your return more likely to be audited. It is also very important to make sure that the contributions you deduct are to *qualified* charities as defined by law: religious, charitable, governmental, educational, and civic organizations recognized as legitimate recipients of tax-deductible contributions. The IRS is aware that tuition may be disguised as a charitable contribution and will look for such violations. The same is true if you report large donations of property and the charitable organization reports to the IRS sale of these items at a value much lower than what you have claimed. Thirteen audited returns in my sample

BE SURE TO DOCUMENT THAT THE MEDICAL EXPENSES YOU CLAIM WERE NOT PAID BY YOUR MEDICAL INSURANCE CARRIER, AND THAT THEY EXCEED 7.5% OF YOUR ADJUSTED GROSS INCOME

MAKE SURE THE RECIPIENTS OF YOU CHARITABLE CONTRIBUTIONS ARE LEGITIMATE AND THAT THE AMOUNTS ARE WITHIN THE LEGAL LIMIT reported questionable charitable contributions. The audits, however, seem to have been caused by a combination of this factor with others.

5. Home Office:

This is an old favorite of the IRS. Home office expenses are reported on Schedule C and the PAR limits we discussed in that context apply. However, the fact that you report a home office may increase your audit probability somewhat beyond the limits we discussed for Schedule C, simply because the IRS likes to question the *reasons* for your having a home office in the first place. There have been many recent legal precedents, some in favor of the IRS, and an agent may be successful in disallowing your home office expenses if it can be argued that you are not entitled to one. Four hundred and eleven of my audits (over two-thirds of the audit sample) included a Schedule C. Of these returns, 289 reported a home office. Of the unaudited returns, 314 had a Schedule C, and 98 of them reported a home office. The audits, however, were all explained by breach of the PAR. I believe that a home office may increase your audit probability *after* your return has been picked by the DIF because you exceeded the PAR limit. Possibly, once this has happened, the classifier may be more likely to decide to audit you once he or she sees that you have reported a home office.

YOUR AUDIT
PROBABILITY WILL
INCREASE IF
YOU EXCEED LIM-
ITS SET BY LAW
ON VARIOUS
DEDUCTIONS,
OR DO
NOT FOLLOW
OTHER LEGAL
GUIDELINES

Chapter 20

CHAPTER 21

HOW THE DIF WAS ESTIMATED

As a statistical discriminant function, the DIF is a rule that separates the population of taxpayers into two groups: one that yields more money following an audit and another that does not. As with all statistical methods, there is a "truth" (population), and a sample-based *estimate*. That is, if we had complete knowledge, we could identify all the people in the *population* of taxpayers who would yield more money on audit. Let's call this sub-population Group M. The taxpayers in the entire population who would *not* yield more money in audit are Group N. Figure 5 below shows the two groups. Now, the DIF is a statistically-derived rule that tries to *find* all of Group M, without including any people from Group N because auditing these people will just cause the government to throw away money conducting audits of people who won't lead to more revenue (or even may require a refund!—an expensive error). Since the rule is a statistical one, it is not perfect, and using the DIF gives the IRS Group A (for "audit") which contains Group M members, but some that are not. This, too, is shown in Figure 5.

Figure 5

THE BOX REPRESENTS ALL TAXPAYERS

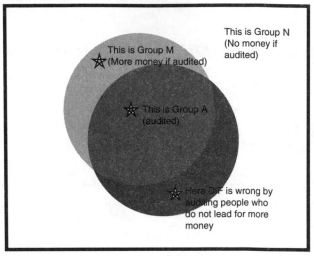

What did I do? I wasn't at all interested in Group M (I don't really care who can yield more money following an audit). I used the same *discriminant function analysis* to try to identify Group A! That is, I tried to find out who gets audited and who doesn't. My estimate, obtained by looking at returns of audited and unaudited taxpayers, is Group B (for "buster"). Since I, too, used statistics, my estimated discriminant function could differ from the "true" one and therefore my Group B does not necessarily coincide exactly with the IRS' Group A, but it is close. This is shown in Figure 6.

Figure 6

THE BOX REPRESENTS ALL TAXPAYERS

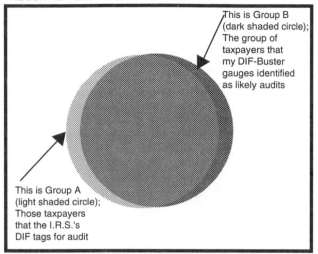

This is Group B
(dark shaded circle);
The group of
taxpayers that
my DIF-Buster
gauges identified
as likely audits

This is Group A
(light shaded circle);
Those taxpayers
that the I.R.S.'s
DIF tags for audit

But here is where some *higher* level mathematics and computing power came in. Since many returns in my unaudited category *could* have been picked up by the IRS' DIF but were then dropped by the classifier who looked at the computer-tagged return, this could have introduced a serious bias into the methodology. The trick now was to look *only* at the audited returns, since they could only have been picked up by the DIF (except for a very small fraction of TCMP audits). Once my own DIF told me which *variables* were statistically significant, the estimation phase was done by considering the audits alone. This was done using a highly sophisticated artificial-intelligence routine that searches for the *minimum* point for an audit based on any of the variables that were identified, and their combinations. The results of the analysis are believed to be quite accurate. While the IRS will never admit this, if one were to look at their infamous DIF, one would find that my formulas are very good estimates of that statistical rule. This was confirmed when I "blindfolded" the computer and asked it to use the estimated rules to classify the returns that I fed it—without the computer knowing whether or not a particular return was audited. Using the PAR rules, the computer did classify correctly over 95% of the returns that I fed it. The validation sample contained 206 returns: 109 audits and 97 no-audits. One-hundred and four of the audits were correctly classified by the computer. For the no-audit group, 92 were correctly classified.

CHAPTER 22

SUMMARY OF AUDIT-PROOFING RULES, AND EXAMPLES

he following is a summary of the things to look for on your return in trying to minimize audit probability.

1. Check for math errors
2. No Nice Numbers
3. No significant inconsistencies across years
4. No large numerical shifts across years
5. Agreement of federal return with state return
6. No breach of legal limits on deductions
7. Explain all questionable items or amounts
8. File late if possible
9. Agreement of information with independent reporting
10. PAR(A) not in Critical Zone, and preferably not in Caution Zone
11. PAR(C) not in Critical Zone, and preferably not in Caution Zone
12. PAR(F) not in Critical Zone, and preferably not in Caution Zone
13. PAR(C) + 1.5 PAR(A) satisfying Caution inequality
14. Check for Red Flags: bad debt, casualty loss.

113

EXAMPLES

The following examples of tax returns are *real*. The names have been changed for obvious reasons. So have the professions, geographical locations, and other details. Small changes were also made in all the numbers involved so that even the IRS will not be able to identify the actual taxpayers whose returns these are. Some actual information, such as spouse's names and other details, have been left out of the forms.

Example (1)

John Greene is a realtor living in Omaha. He is married with no dependent children; his wife is retired. John's return is shown below. Was John's return audited?

Form **1040**	Department of the Treasury—Internal Revenue Service U.S. **Individual Income Tax Return** (0) 19		IRS Use Only—Do not write or staple in this space.
	For the year Jan. 1–Dec. 31, 1993, or other tax year beginning	, 1993, ending . 19	OMB No. 1545-0074
Label (See instructions on page 12.) Use the IRS bel.	Your first name and initial Last name John W. Greene		Your social security number
	If a joint return, spouse's first name and initial Last name		Spouse's social security number
	Home address (number and street). If you have a P.O. box, see page 12.	Apt. no.	For Privacy Act an Paperwork P Act No*
	City, town or post office, state, and ZIP code. If you have a foreign address, see page 12.		Y

	~nt $3 to go to this fund? . . . . ~spouse want *~ ~n *			
	~ner incon.. ~ist type ano amount—see page 20		**22**	
	23 Add the amounts in the far right column for lines 7 through 22. This is your **total income** ▶		**23**	23,670
Adjustments to Income (See page 20.)	**24a** Your IRA deduction (see page 20)	**24a**		
	b Spouse's IRA deduction (see page 20)	**24b**		
	25 One-half of self-employment tax (see page 21) . . .	**25**	42	
	26 Self-employed health insurance deduction (see page 22)	**26**		
	27 Keogh retirement plan and self-employed SEP deduction	**27**		
	28 Penalty on early withdrawal of savings	**28**		
	29 Alimony paid. Recipient's SSN ▶	**29**		
	30 Add lines 24a through 29. These are your **total adjustments** . . . . ▶		**30**	42
Adjusted Gross Income	**31** Subtract line 30 from line 23. This is your **adjusted gross income.** *If this amount is less than $23,050 and a child lived with you, see page EIC-1 to find out if you can claim the "Earned Income Credit" on line 56* . . . . ▶		**31**	23,628

Cat. No. 11320B   Form **1040** (1993)

Schedule A—Itemized Deductions

(Schedule B is on back)

▶ Attach to Form 1040. ▶ See Instructions for Schedules A and B (Form 1040).

OMB No. 1545-0074

19

Attachment
Sequence No. **07**

Name(s) shown on Form 1040   Your social security number

John W. Greene

~~not include expenses reimbursed or paid by others.~~   4,___   25

	26	Is the amount on Form 1040, line 32, more than $108,450 (more than $54,225 if		
Itemized Deductions		married filing separately)?		

- **NO.** Your deduction is not limited. Add lines 4, 8, 12, 16, 17, 18, 24, and 25 and enter the total here. Also enter on Form 1040, line 34, the **larger** of this amount or your standard deduction.   } ▶ | 26 | 8,409 |
- **YES.** Your deduction may be limited. See page A-5 for the amount to enter.

For Paperwork Reduction Act Notice, see Form 1040 Instructions.   Cat. No. 11330X   Schedule A (Form 1040) 1993

Profit or Loss From Business

(Sole Proprietorship)

▶ Partnerships, joint ventures, etc., must file Form 1065.

▶ Attach to Form 1040 or Form 1041. ▶ See Instructions for Schedule C (Form 1040).

OMB No. 1545-0074

19

Attachment
Sequence No. **09**

Name of proprietor   Social security number (SSN)

John W. Greene

~~~ssion~~ including product or service (see page C-1)   B Enter prir

17	~~Legal ~ professi~~ services	17		27	Other expenses (from line 46 on page 2)	27	2,163
18	Office expense	18					
28	Total expenses before expenses for business use of home. Add lines 8 through 27 in columns. . ▶					28	3,182
29	Tentative profit (loss). Subtract line 28 from line 7					29	598
30	Expenses for business use of your home. Attach Form 8829					30	0
31	Net profit or (loss). Subtract line 30 from line 29.						

- If a profit, enter on **Form 1040, line 12,** and ALSO on **Schedule SE, line 2** (statutory employees, see page C-5). Fiduciaries, enter on Form 1041, line 3.   } | 31 | 598 |
- If a loss, you MUST go on to line 32.

32	If you have a loss, check the box that describes your investment in this activity (see page C-5).		

- If you checked 32a, enter the loss on **Form 1040, line 12,** and ALSO on **Schedule SE, line 2** (statutory employees), see page C-5. Fiduciaries, enter on Form 1041, line 3.   }
- If you checked 32b, you MUST attach **Form 6198.**

32a ☐ All investment is at risk.
32b ☐ Some investment is not at risk.

For Paperwork Reduction Act Notice, see Form 1040 Instructions.   Cat. No. 11334P   Schedule C (Form 1040) 1993

Example (2)

Denise Burns is a civil engineer living with her husband, Michael, in New York City. Their return is shown below. Was this return audited?

Form **1040**	Department of the Treasury—Internal Revenue Service **U.S. Individual Income Tax Return** (O) 19		IRS Use Only—Do not write or staple in this space.
	For the year Jan. 1–Dec. 31, 1993, or other tax year beginning , 1993, ending , 19		OMB No. 1545-0074

Label
(See instructions on page 12.)
Use the IRS

Your first name and initial Denise M.	Last name Burns		Your social security number
If a joint return, spouse's first name and initial	Last name		Spouse's social security number
Home address (number and street). If you have a P.O. box, see page 12.		Apt. no.	

	21a Social security benefits 21a		b Taxable amount (see page ..)		
	22 Other income. List type and amount—see page 20			**22**	1,905
	23 Add the amounts in the far right column for lines 7 through 22. This is your **total income** ▶			**23**	49,926

Adjustments to Income
(See page 20.)

24a Your IRA deduction (see page 20)	**24a**		
b Spouse's IRA deduction (see page 20)	**24b**		
25 One-half of self-employment tax (see page 21) . . .	**25**	73	
26 Self-employed health insurance deduction (see page 22)	**26**		
27 Keogh retirement plan and self-employed SEP deduction	**27**		
28 Penalty on early withdrawal of savings	**28**		
29 Alimony paid. Recipient's SSN ▶	**29**		
30 Add lines 24a through 29. These are your **total adjustments** . . . . ▶		**30**	73

Adjusted Gross Income

31 Subtract line 30 from line 23. This is your **adjusted gross income.** If this amount is less than $23,050 and a child lived with you, see page EIC-1 to find out if you can claim the "Earned Income Credit" on line 56 . . . . ▶		**31**	49,853

Cat. No. 11320B   Form **1040** (1993)

Schedule A—Itemized Deductions

(Schedule B is on back)

Department of the Treasury
Internal Revenue Service   (O)   ▶ **Attach to Form 1040.** ▶ **See Instructions for Schedules A and B (Form 1040).**

OMB No. 1545-0074

19

Attachment
Sequence No. **07**

Name(s) shown on Form 1040   Denise M. Burns

Your social security number

	...(include ~~ed or paid~~				
24	Subtract ...e 23 from ... n zero or less, enter -0-				
Other Miscellaneous Deductions 25	Other—from list on page A-5. List type and amount ▶				
	....	▶	**25**		
Total Itemized Deductions 26	Is the amount on Form 1040, line 32, more than $108,450 (more than $54,225 if married filing separately)?				
	● **NO.** Your deduction is not limited. Add lines 4, 8, 12, 16, 17, 18, 24, and 25 and enter the total here. Also enter on Form 1040, line 34, the **larger** of this amount or your standard deduction.	} ▶	**26**	6,461	
	● **YES.** Your deduction may be limited. See page A-5 for the amount to enter.				

For Paperwork Reduction Act Notice, see Form 1040 instructions.   Cat. No. 11330X   Schedule A (Form 1040) 1993

Profit or Loss From Business

(Sole Proprietorship)

▶ **Partnerships, joint ventures, etc., must file Form 1065.**

Department of the Treasury
Internal Revenue Service   (O)   ▶ **Attach to Form 1040 or Form 1041.** ▶ **See Instructions for Schedule C (Form 1040).**

OMB No. 1545-0074

19

Attachment
Sequence No. **09**

Name of proprietor   Denise M. Burns

Social security number (SSN)

A   ~ipal business or profession. including produ~ ~~ ~~

	Legal ~ ~ressional services	**17**	2,241	**27** Other expenses (from line 46 on	~~ ~~		
18	Office expense	**18**		page 2)	**27**	8,227	
28	Total expenses before expenses for business use of home. Add lines 8 through 27 in columns ▶				**28**	44,407	
29	Tentative profit (loss). Subtract line 28 from line 7				**29**	1,024	
30	Expenses for business use of your home. Attach **Form 8829**				**30**	0	
31	**Net profit or (loss).** Subtract line 30 from line 29.						
	● If a profit, enter on **Form 1040, line 12,** and ALSO on **Schedule SE, line 2** (statutory employees, see page C-5). Fiduciaries, enter on Form 1041, line 3.				**31**	1,024	}
	● If a loss, you MUST go on to line 32.						
32	If you have a loss, check the box that describes your investment in this activity (see page C-5).						
	● If you checked 32a, enter the loss on **Form 1040, line 12,** and ALSO on **Schedule SE, line 2** (statutory employees, see page C-5). Fiduciaries, enter on Form 1041, line 3.				**32a** ☐ All investment is at risk.		}
	● If you checked 32b, you MUST attach **Form 6198.**				**32b** ☐ Some investment is not at risk.		

For Paperwork Reduction Act Notice, see Form 1040 instructions.   Cat. No. 11334P   Schedule C (Form 1040) 1993

Answers: Both John and Denise were audited. John's PAR(C) is high: 84.2%, which is past the critical point of 67%. His PAR(A) is 35.6%, which is just at the start of the caution zone for PAR(A). The combined score is: PAR(C)+1.5PAR(A)=137.6%, which is also in the bad zone. Most likely, John's high PAR(C) is the cause of the audit. Denise's PAR(C) is 98%, way past the critical point, but her PAR(A) is in the safe zone at 13%. At 117.5%, her combined ratio is also in the bad zone. She was definitely audited because of her high PAR(C).

CHAPTER 23

COMPUTING YOUR AUDIT PROBABILITY

I would prefer to have you compute the PARs in the previous chapters, as well as check all the other factors that affect your return and change things that are under your control, such as provide documentation, file late if you can, etc. Some people, however, would like to be able to compute the actual probability of an audit for a given return. While I am reluctant to provide you with the methodology to do so, because audit probabilities can be deceiving, I will do so in this chapter. Keep in mind, however, that some probabilities may seem small to you—after all, the IRS only audits about one percent of all returns—and that you need to look at these probabilities as *relative quantities*. If you compute your audit probability and it comes out to be 18%, do *not* rejoice at it being "so small." It is not! Eighteen percent is eighteen times higher than the overall national average! It also means that you will be audited (on *average*) roughly once in a little over five years. Do not approach your tax return preparation as a night in a casino! Having said all this, let's see how the probability of an audit can be computed.

STEP ONE:

We will start with the IRS's own reported overall audit probabilities, by state. These are given in Table 2 below. Use the appropriate number from the table that corresponds to your state as your *starting value.* (If you live in Pennsylvania, your starting value is 0.69%, or 0.0069 if you like to write it decimally.)

Table 2

Audit-Probabilities by State (%)

(In Decreasing Order)

Alaska	2.46	Missouri	0.81
Nevada	1.89	Alabama	0.80
Wyoming	1.68	Indiana	0.77
Utah	1.61	Mississippi	0.77
Oklahoma	1.45	Oregon	0.77
N. Dakota	1.40	Vermont	0.77
Texas	1.36	Tennessee	0.76
California	1.31	Florida	0.74
Washington	1.20	S. Dakota	0.72
Montana	1.11	Connecticut	0.71
Colorado	1.07	Louisiana	0.71
Arizona	1.03	W. Virginia	0.71
Kansas	0.95	Pennsylvania	0.69
Idaho	0.94	Michigan	0.67
Hawaii	0.93	Virginia	0.64
Georgia	0.93	S. Carolina	0.64
Illinois	0.93	Arkansas	0.63
New Mexico	0.93	Kentucky	0.63
Ohio	0.90	New Jersey	0.62
Minnesota	0.89	Iowa	0.60
New York	0.89	N. Carolina	0.60
Delaware	0.86	New Hampshire	0.59
Nebraska	0.85	Wisconsin	0.59
Maryland (and	0.81	Massachusetts	0.58
District of Columbia)		Rhode Island	0.57
		Maine	0.55

(Compiled from: IRS Commissioner Annual Reports; *Statistics of Income Bulletin,* IRS)

STEP TWO:
If you are filing the "EZ" form, multiply your probability by
0.1. Your audit probability is minimal. If you are filing the
short form, 1040A, multiply your probability by 0.4.

STEP THREE:
If you have a Schedule C, *multiply your starting value by
4.5.* For example, suppose you live in Idaho, so your starting value is 0.94. If you have a Schedule C, multiply: 0.94
x 4.5 = 4.23%.

If you have a Schedule F, multiple your starting value by
2.1. If you live in Iowa and are filing a Schedule F, your
probability is now 0.60 x 2.1 = 1.26%. If you have both
Schedules C and F, multiply your starting value by both 4.5
and 2.1.

STEP FOUR:
For every PAR that exceeds the critical point, multiply your
probability by 4. Continuing the Schedule C example
above, suppose that your PAR(C) is 98.5%, which exceeds
the critical point of 67%. You therefore multiply your
probability by 4, getting: 4.23 x 4 = 16.92%. If you also
have a Schedule A and it is beyond the critical point for
PAR(A), you need to multiply again by 4. You do not have
to consider the *combined* test for PAR(A) and PAR(C) in
these multiplications.

If your PAR for a given schedule is in the caution zone, not
beyond the critical point, multiply your probability by 1.5.

In the example above, suppose you only have a Schedule C and that your PAR(C) is 60%, then you multiply: 4.23 x 1.5 = 6.345%.

If your PAR for a given schedule is in the safe zone (less than the caution point), multiply your probability by 0.3. In our example, suppose there is only a Schedule C and that PAR(C)=18%. The probability now is 4.23 x 0.3 = 1.27%.

STEP FIVE:

For every page of supplemental documentation you pro-vide (quality is subjective and hard to give fast rules for, so the following is very general and assumes high quality), multiply your probability by 0.9. This holds for up to 10 pages. Thereafter, still multiply by 0.9 only 10 times. Suppose that your probability by the previous step is 16.92% and that you provide 5 neat pages of explanations for your deductions. Your probability is now: 16.92 x 0.9 x 0.9 x 0.9 x 0.9 x 0.9 = 9.99%. Your audit probability is roughly 10%.

STEP SIX:

If you get one extension to file in August, multiply your probability by 0.6. If you then get another extension to file in October, multiply your probability *again* by 0.6. In the example above, suppose you start with 9.99% audit proba-bility and get two extensions so you can file by October 15, your final audit probability is: 9.99 x 0.6 x 0.6 = 3.6%.

FINAL STEP:

If there are any other factors affecting your return, red flags or other, the probability will be increased.

Remember that these are rough rules and that probability interpretations may be deceiving. Try to work on your return without pinning down a number for the audit probability. Use the quality-control approach of checking all details that lead to inflated PARs and other factors that may flag your return. When these are unavoidable, explain!

CHAPTER 24

TAX SHELTERS

A tax shelter is a method or transaction or investment that gives tax benefits to the participant. The IRS code is designed to give us the opportunity to benefit from *legitimate* tax shelters—those that have redeeming social and/or economic value as recognized by Congress. The idea behind the law is to encourage certain kinds of investments even though the government pays for them by having reduced tax revenues. Your home is a tax shelter, since your mortgage interest and taxes are deductible. Many tax shelters are business ventures in which accounting losses far exceed the accounting income. The losses are then used to offset other income and thus shield it from taxation. Our economy requires large investments in farming, mining, oil and gas drilling, building, etc., and the purpose of the law reducing the tax is to allow the formation of such businesses that require large initial investment. Tax shelters usually have at least one of the following characteristics:

1. Taxes are deferred to later years.
2. Ordinary gains are converted to capital gains.
3. Leverage is used.

Clearly, there is great potential for abuse. An *abusive tax shelter*, as the IRS defines it, is a scheme that involves artificial transactions with little or no economic value, and whose sole purpose is to reduce the participant's tax bill. Often an abusive tax shelter will involve a package deal that is designed from the start to generate losses, deductions, or credits.

THE IRS VIGOROUSLY HUNTS DOWN ABUSIVE TAX SHELTERS

A number of the audits in my sample seem to have been picked up because the taxpayer participated in an abusive tax shelter. The IRS also likes to make an example of people participating in such tax shelters. In a crackdown on abusive tax shelters a few years ago, a number of Hollywood personalities were investigated and penalized for participating in one such scheme. Often such schemes are marketed in a way that hides their true nature, and you will want to be careful before you invest.

It is very unlikely that the DIF itself has some mechanism that can identify an abusive tax shelter as opposed to a legitimate one. In most probability, it is the classifier who, looking at your return once it is identified by the DIF for other reasons, may suspect an abusive tax shelter and make the decision to audit you. Remember that it really doesn't matter whether or not your tax shelter is abusive. What counts is what the IRS agent or classifier will *think* it is, and that will determine whether or not you are audited.

YOU DO NOT WANT TO HAVE A TAX SHELTER THAT THE IRS WILL THINK IS AN ABUSIVE ONE

What does the IRS look for in determining that a tax shelter is abusive? IRS agents are trained to look for the following telltales in checking for abusive tax shelters:

1. Investments made late in the tax year.
2. A very large portion of the investment is made in the first year.
3. Burden and benefit of ownership is not passed to the taxpayer.
4. The sale price does not compare well with fair market value.
5. Estimated present value of future income does not compare well with present value of all investment and associated costs.

According to the IRS, most abusive tax shelters are in the following areas: real estate, oil and gas, farming, motion pictures, videotapes, commodities, master recordings, leasing, cable TV, mining, foreign trusts. The IRS has a special Tax Shelter Program designed to combat abusive tax shelters. You will want to be very careful in preparing your return to avoid falling into the category of people audited for tax shelter abuse. Audits of tax shelter abuse result in an average annual additional tax collection of over 2.5 billion dollars.

As a final quality-control check of your return before submitting it, check for the above signs that the IRS considers significant in determining that a tax shelter is abusive. If you have investments in any of the areas listed above, and if your investment has any of the features that auditors look for, you will do well to include ample documentation to explain the investment so the classifier does not decide to audit you.

CHAPTER 25

A WAY (FOR SOME) TO HAVE
A FINAL LAUGH

When you file your tax return you sign a statement saying that, under penalty of perjury, you have told the truth as accurately as possible. The following should only be interpreted in this context.

Suppose that you filed your return, as accurately as possible at the time of filing, but later discovered that you left out some item or items that would reduce your tax liability. To take advantage of these new facts, you want to refile your tax return. This is possible, and such a return is called an *amended* return, and is filed on Form 1040X. An amended return is also possible in case you have been audited and as a result of your audit you were charged additional tax. Regardless of whether or not you appealed, you ended up paying that additional tax. Now, some time later, you discover some new facts and evidence that you believe will entitle you to some deductions that the auditor had disallowed. You may now file an amended return to recover your money.

Amended returns impact very strongly on your chance of being audited. The first fact we need to mention is that, in general, filing an amended return will increase your probability of an audit. For some reason, the IRS looks at amended returns more sternly. The Service believes that more abuse may be possible with amended returns and instructs its agents to audit more often. The two rules mentioned in a previous chapter about decreases in tax liability beyond certain limits for schedules B and D requiring an audit are good examples of this.

There is a more important point here, however, which works very strongly in *your favor*. This point—as is the case with many topics in this book—has to do with *time*. For some odd reason, an aberration in the tax law exists. The period of time for the IRS to collect more tax from you expires, as we said earlier, after three years from the date the tax was due (usually April 15th of the year you file, although note our earlier comments on the exceptions). Now, your time period for requesting a refund for a particular tax year is also three years from the time you filed (assuming you filed April 15), regardless of any extensions you may have obtained. There are two exceptions to this rule. First, if your revision involves a bad debt or a worthless security, you have up to seven years to file an amended return. Second, you may file for a refund up to two years from the last date *tax was paid for the year*, but the refund amount is limited to no more than the amount of tax paid on that latest date. For example, if you were audited and had to pay more tax, say two years after filing, you can file for a refund up to two years from that last date you paid tax (that is, four years after the original return was filed), but the amount of refund is limited to the amount of tax you paid at that latest date.

Here comes your incredible advantage. While you have all this time to file for a refund, the IRS is *still limited* by the time limit valid for your *original* return, and cannot ask you for more tax for the year once the original time limit of three years has expired.

Suppose you filed your return for 1993 on April 15, 1994, and a few months later discovered that you failed to make a deduction that would have reduced your tax for 1993 by several thousand dollars. The best thing for you to do is to *wait* until a few days before April 15, 1997 (that is, a few days before time runs out on you for requesting a refund) and then file an amended return for 1993 claiming the deduction. The IRS may disallow your claim, or reduce the amount, or it may pay you in full. At any rate, once April 15, 1997 arrives, it *cannot* ask you for more tax for 1993 because the period of limitations will have expired. Filing a few days before April 15, 1997, puts you within the time limit for a refund, and yet makes it almost impossible for the IRS to audit your 1993 return and ask for more tax—all in a few days before the deadline passes. This is demonstrated in figure 7.

Out of 58 amended returns in my sample, 39 were audited. Of the nineteen unaudited amended returns, seven were filed within two months of the date time would have run out on the IRS for conducting an audit of the original return.

Figure 7

The time element and amended returns

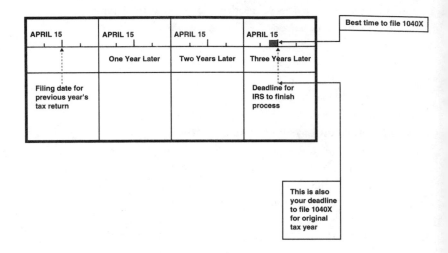

BY CLEVERLY TIMING YOUR REQUEST FOR A REFUND YOU CAN MAKE IT ALMOST IMPOSSIBLE FOR THE IRS TO AUDIT YOUR ORIGINAL RETURN AND ASK FOR MORE TAX

Chapter 25

This technique can also be used quite well after an audit. You pay the additional tax assessed in the audit (assuming you were unable to reverse the assessment in appeals or court), you wait for the time to run out completely on the IRS for asking for more tax—three years from the time you filed—but no later than two years after the audit. Then you file for a refund. This assumes that you can present some newly discovered reason for asking for the refund: something in your favor that was overlooked in the audit, or something that does not have to do with the audit— some other item or items in the original return. The IRS cannot audit you again, in the sense that the period allowing it to ask for more tax for that year is over. In such cases, the maximum amount you claim as refund is the last amount of tax paid, the additional tax assessed in the audit.

Of the returns in my sample, none were assessed more tax or even audited if the amended return was filed within two weeks of the day time ran out on the IRS to assess more tax. Remember that the amended return itself may not result in the amount of refund you request, but timing will minimize exposure of the rest of your return to an audit. Playing the amended return game can be dangerous and tricky, but to the shrewd and lucky it can be quite rewarding.

CHAPTER 26

APPENDIX—The Taxpayer Bill of Rights

Enacted by Congress in 1988, the Taxpayer Bill of Rights is designed to offer some protection to us taxpayers against the all-powerful Goliath. This chapter summarizes some of the more important rights provided by the law. The most important protection in the bill is the establishment of an Ombudsman to protect the taxpayers. Usually, the Ombudsman works through the IRS' Problem Resolution Offices that are part of each District Office. Here, problems with the Service may be worked out. The Ombudsman may issue a Taxpayer Assistance Order (TAO), which can stop the seizure of property or wages. To get a TAO, the taxpayer must apply to the Problem Resolution Office and show that significant hardship will result from the IRS action. Other important rights are:

1. A Notice of Taxpayer's Rights must be mailed to the taxpayer with the first IRS notice about delinquent taxes. This is an important publication.

2. Taxpayers' Rights during non-criminal IRS interviews are:
a) The right to make an audio recording of the

interview. The taxpayer must notify the agent that a recording is being made and give the IRS a chance to do the same.

b) A taxpayer may send a qualified representative to meet with the agent instead of him- or herself.

c) At any time during the interview, the taxpayer may request an end to the meeting to have an opportunity to consult with a tax professional.

d) The IRS is now required to consider the taxpayer when setting times and places for interviews.

3. If a taxpayer relied on bad IRS *written* advice, penalties may be removed.

4. IRS production quotas are officially forbidden. This means that the auditor's performance is not supposed to be evaluated based on the amount of tax dollars he or she collects.

5. A taxpayer may *propose* to the IRS an installment payment plan. However, the IRS is not obligated to accept the plan, only to consider it.

6. A Notice of Levy must be given to the taxpayer prior to property seizure, giving the taxpayer 30 days to contest or negotiate to stop the levy.

7. Erroneous tax liens may be appealed to the

Ombudsman.

8. The taxpayer has the right to sue the IRS for up to $100.000 plus legal costs if IRS collection personnel have intentionally disregarded the law. Stringent provisions, however, apply to protect the IRS.

YOU CAN HELP!

The research that has gone into developing this book was a monumental effort. The crucial element was the collection of tax returns of audited versus unaudited taxpayers. Future editions of this book will depend on the availability of ample new data.

IF YOU HAVE BEEN AUDITED IN RECENT YEARS, I WOULD GREATLY APPRECIATE RECEIVING A COPY OF YOUR AUDITED RETURN.

To reward your participation, I will run your present year return through the computer program and tell you what to watch out for. I will also compute your audit probability. Please send your audited return to:

Professor Amir D. Aczel
Department of Mathematical Sciences
Bentley College
Waltham, MA 02154

Thank you!

BIBLIOGRAPHY

Aczel, Amir D., *Complete Business Statistics*, 2d ed., Burr Ridge, IL: Irwin, 1993. (Chapter 16 of my book gives a thorough explanation of discriminant analysis.)

American Statistical Association, *Proceedings of the Joint Statistical Meetings, San Francisco*, Arlington, VA: American Statistical Association, 1993. (Various papers by IRS statisticians.)

Bernstein, Allen, *Tax Guide for College Teachers*, Washington, DC: Academic Information Service, 1992.

Burnham, David, *A Law Unto Itself: Power, Politics, and the IRS*, New York: Random House, 1990. (The title says it all.)

Commerce Clearing House Tax Law Editors, *Federal Tax Course*, Chicago: Commerce Clearing House, 1990.

Daily, Frederick W., *Winning the IRS Game: How Anyone Can Beat the IRS*, San Francisco: Dropzone Press, 1991. (A tax attorney reveals some of his trade secrets.)

Diogenes, *The April Game: Secrets of an Internal Revenue Agent*, Chicago: The Playboy Press, 1973.

Gates, Bryan E., *How to Represent Your Client Before the IRS*, New York: McGraw-Hill, 1983. (A guide for tax professionals, with useful advice.)

Huberty, Carl J., *Applied Discriminant Analysis*, New York: Wiley, 1994. (An excellent guide to understanding discriminant analysis.)

Internal Revenue Service Commissioner's *Annual Report*, Washington, DC: U.S. Department of the Treasury, 1991.

Internal Revenue Service Commissioner's *Annual Report*, Washington, DC: U.S. Department of the Treasury, 1992.

Internal Revenue Service, *Statistics of Income Bulletin*, Washington, DC: U.S. Department of the Treasury, Vol. 13, Numbers 1 and 2, 1993.

Internal Revenue Service, *Statistics of Income Bulletin*, Washington, DC: U.S. Department of the Treasury, Vol. 12, Number 1, 1992.

Internal Revenue Service, *Your Federal Income Tax: for Individuals* (Publication 17), Washington, DC: U.S. Department of the Treasury, 1993. (The IRS's guide for individuals preparing their taxes.)

Larson, Martin A., *The IRS vs. the Middle Class*, Old Greenwich, CT: Devin-Adair, 1980.

Lasser, J. K., *Your Income Tax*, New York: Prentice-Hall, 1993. (A classic guide for preparing your taxes.)

McCormally, Kevin, *Sure Ways to Cut Your Taxes*, Washington DC: Kiplinger, 1994. (A friendly, sometimes humorous guide to preparing your taxes.)

Norusis, Marija J., *SPSS Advanced Statistics Guide*, Chicago: SPSS, 1990. (A statistical guide to computing a discriminant function, such as the IRS' "DIF".)

Phillips, Lawrence C., and John L. Kramer, eds., *Federal Taxation*, New York: Prentice-Hall, 1990.

Schnepper, Jeff A., *Inside IRS: How Internal Revenue Works (You Over)*, New York: Stein and Day, 1978.

Schnepper, Jeff A., *How to Pay Zero Taxes*, New York: McGraw-Hill, 1994. (A good guide to federal taxation, notwithstanding its misleading title.)

Stern, Philip M., *The Rape of the Taxpayer*, New York: Random House, 1973.

Sydlaske, Janet M., and Richard K. Millcroft, *The Only Tax Audit Guide You'll Ever Need*, New York: Wiley, 1990. (Advice on handling your audit.)

Wade, Jack W., *Audit-Proofing Your Return*, New York: Macmillan, 1986.

Whitley, Roger, *Assess the IRS!*, New York: Vantage Press, 1978. (A hair-raising story of an endless audit.)

INDEX

A

Alternative Minimum Tax (AMT)   32
Amended return   127-31
American Statistical Association   28
Appeals (audit)   69
Artificial intelligence   81
Audits by IRS   1
Automated Collection System (ACS)   74
Avoiding audits   79

C

Canceled checks   49
Capone, Al   14
Caution Point   95
Caution Zone   95
Charitable contributions   107
Classification of taxpayers   23
Clinton, Bill   15
Cohan rule   65
Collection Division, IRS   11
Combination of Schedules   103
Compliance 2000 program (IRS)   29
Computer, IRS, in West Virginia   7, 8
        Worship by IRS personnel   8
Courts   73
Cray-2 supercomputer   4
Criminal Investigations Division (CID)   11, 44
Critical Point   95
Critical Zone   95

D

Deadline for audits	37-38
Delay in filing return	83
DIF-Buster Gauge	96
Schedule A	96-98
Schedule C	99-100
Schedule F	101-102
Discriminant Analysis	23, 24
Discriminant Function (DIF)	9, 10, 24, 110
District Office, IRS	11

E

Entrapping by IRS	43
Errors in entering returns	8
Examination Division, IRS	11
Extension of time for IRS	41

F

Fear of IRS	14-15
Fisher, Sir Ronald A.	25
Field Audit	11
Form 1040A	120
1040EZ	120
1040X	126
872	41
4868	83
2688	83

G

General Accounting Office (GAO)	3

H

Helmsley, Leona   14-15
Hidden income   56
Hobby, determination by IRS   67
Home office   108

I

Information element (audits)   42
IRS   1
    Audits   1
    Manual   12
    Headquarters   7
    Service Center   7

J

Jeopardy Assessment   75

K

Keypunch operators   7

M

Miranda protection   13
Money magazine   10

N

Nice Numbers Trap   9
Nonfiler   15

O

Office Audit   11
Ombudsman   131
Open year   62

Overdeductor 18

P

Personal Accounting Ratio (PAR) 91
    Schedule A 91-92
    Schedule C 93
    Schedule F 94
Probability of audit 118-22
    By State 119
Problem Resolution Office (PRO), IRS 11
Psychology, use in audit 34

Q

Quality control 81

R

Random sample of taxpayers 22
Red flags 106
Regional Commissioner, IRS 7
Rewards by IRS for information 18-19

S

Santa Vittoria 20
Schedule A 91
Schedule B 105
Schedule C 93
Schedule D 106
Schedule F 94
Secret Formula, IRS 2, 10
Service Centers, IRS 7
Settlement with IRS 71
Social Security Number (SSN) 8

Statistical profile, taxpayer   9
Statisticians, IRS   25
Statistics   4
Supercomputer   4
Supplements, tax return   88-90

T

Tax collector   74
Taxpayer   1
Taxpayer Bill of Rights   131-33
Taxpayer Compliance Measurement Program
(TCMP)   21
Tax Professionals   43-46
Tax return   4
30-Day-Letter   70
Time element, in audits   37-42
        Amended returns   127

U

Underreporter   16

Chapter 1

146